CELEBRATE
Freedom!
Christian Singles Learning To Heal

KATHERINE HARGROVE

CELEBRATE FREEDOM
Katherine Hargrove

Requests for information should be directed to:
ZizaCreative Publishing, Inc.
718-708-3348
New York

Cover & Interior Layout by StudioNouveauNYC.com

ISBN 979-8-218-03092-6

Unless otherwise noted, all scripture references are taken
from the King James Version of the Bible.

Disclaimers: [1]*The opinions addressed by the author are
exclusively those of the author and in no way express
the convictions of this publishing company.*
[2]*Neither the author nor publisher are liable
or responsible for any outcome that results
from any counseling sessions.*

ZizaCreative
PUBLISHING, INC.

DEDICATION

This book is dedicated to my amazing Heavenly Father who is the only dad I've ever known. Thank you for your bountiful love, abundant help in time of need, genuine concern for my well-being, and extended mercy and grace when I mess up. Thank you for healing every disappointment and for protecting my delicate heart. You are always there for me and consistent in keeping your word to me. Without you this book would not be possible. I'm truly grateful for your wonderful guidance! I love you!

This book is also dedicated to every single person, whether you desire to be married or remain unmarried, who has been hurt, disappointed, weary and discouraged on this incredible journey of singleness. Keep striving, reaching, running, pressing, climbing and progressing forward. Keep living for God! Stay encouraged!

He has not forgotten you!

Acknowledgements

The staff of ZizaCreative Publishing wishes to acknowledge this amazing author, Katherine Hargrove for her stalwart dedication to this project.

This journey began before the pandemic and thank God we are able to bring it to completion so that it can get into the hands of readers. We are certain that everyone who picks up a copy of this book will not only be encouraged but challenged to enjoy their singleness as they wait on the Lord.

This book, CELEBRATE FREEDOM, would not be possible without the concerted faithfulness of our secretaries, doctrinal editors, content and copy editors, editors in chief, proofreaders, design and layout editors. Thanks for your untiring press to move this great work to completion.

CONTENTS

Dedication

Acknowledgment

Part I
The Prison Door is Open: We Are Free!

Part II
Looking Back: Reasons We Go Back

Part III:
The Prison Door is Closed:
Living Free and Staying Free

Part I

The Prison Door is Open
We Are Free!

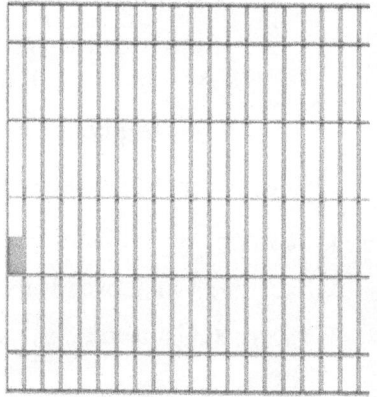

CHAPTER ONE
-FREEDOM -

But joyful are those who have the God of Israel as their helper,
whose hope is in the Lord their God. He made heaven and earth,
the sea and everything in them. He keeps every promise forever.
He gives justice to the oppressed and food to the
hungry. The Lord frees the prisoners.
Psalm 146:5-7 (NLT)

WE LIVE IN a multicultural world made up of people of diverse backgrounds, ethnicities and childhood experiences. In the midst of our unique blends and distinct preferences, there is yet a common pursuit we can probably all agree on. We are in pursuit of joy, hope and freedom. Who wants to feel sad, hopeless and trapped? If we look to our great Lord for help the wonderful result will be joy, hope and freedom. Many of us seek after things (or people) that we believe will produce these three golden elements. However, many times the "things" we are pursuing do not necessarily prove to be the best choice for our well-being; especially when it comes to relationships.

Very often it is a challenge to live as a single person in a society that seems to primarily cater to couples. Such a concept can drive one to open up his/her delicate heart to a person, who does not have his/her best interest in mind, just to be in a relationship with someone. Of course one can always recover from a wounded heart but the scars can be devastating.

If we seek to maintain a relationship with the Lord we will see that He truly "remains faithful forever" as the scripture indicates. What human relationship can offer such a guarantee? Regardless of a person's marital status in life, one can have a wonderful experience in a committed relationship with the "Maker of Heaven, earth and the sea." Sometimes it is hard to wrap the human mind around such a concept; especially when one has been single for a long time. The longer the wait, the more intense the struggle becomes to continue to be hopeful for a mate.

Think about Abraham and Sarah. The struggle to keep believing that she would ever get pregnant and have a son became more intense the longer Sarah had to wait. She grew weary. Sarah lost hope and eventually came up with her own idea to get a son. Unfortunately, this proved to produce some unpleasant consequences *(Genesis 16:1-6, 12)*. What are some things we can learn from this? First, it is important to keep trusting God and maintain our hope in Him. Second, in the midst of our waiting time we should be mindful of the choices we make.

Every now and then in the midst of our singleness we may have moments when we don't feel joy because we do not have a spouse. At times we may spiral downward to a place of weariness because we have been single for so long we have lost hope of ever experiencing marriage. Or maybe we have not been single that long, but really would like to be with someone special. We don't want to be too picky. At the same time we do not want to settle for just anybody flashing pretty white teeth behind a friendly smile either. Sometimes there is a serpent behind the smile.

Very often, in an effort not to live a compromising life, we may sometimes determine it's best not to be around certain people, go to certain places or participate in certain activities. Bad company corrupts good morals. We should be cautious of the company we keep and mindful of the activities we involve ourselves in. While this may be a good thing to consider, it can at times make one feel like he/she is trapped in a cage like a prisoner. In our singleness we may be diligently serving Christ but not really feeling free at all. There should be a healthy balance that does not compromise our relationship with the Lord.

One may ask, "If God is my help, why do I not feel joyful? If my trust is in the Lord then why am I not hopeful? If The Lord has freed the prisoners, then why do I sometimes still feel confined?" Psalm 146:5-7 is just one of many scriptures that convey a message of liberation for those who were once held captive as prisoners. So what exactly does it mean to be a prisoner set free?

The wonderful thing about this scripture is that it reminds us of who we were before our surrender to Christ: prisoners. It also informs us of the only authority qualified to release us: the Lord. A prisoner is one who is confined, bound or held captive by another. The individual is subject to the authority and rules of the one imprisoning him or her.

When you and I were confined to the lure of sin and powerless to overcome it on our own, we were lost souls bound by sin's power and held captive by the authority of our sinful nature. Many of us willingly obeyed the "voice" of our human side and helplessly gave in to its detrimental cravings. Christ, however, was the only hope. In fact He still is the only hope. Yes...the forgiving and merciful judge "pardoned our crimes" and released us from the prison cell within. He has freed us!

He set us free by giving us supernatural power to resist the lure of sin and power to overcome the other "voice" that sometimes influences our decisions. We can now experience freedom from detrimental patterns of behavior and toxic relationships. Before surrendering to Christ, there wasn't much conviction for our lifestyle choices. Obedience to our loving Creator was a foreign concept to some of us. Many of us were partakers of toxic relationships, unhealthy activities and destructive habits. In short, you and I did what we wanted to do, when we wanted to do it and how often we felt like doing it. Why? Because it felt good to us at the time and fulfilled either a real or assumed need. In fact, many of the things some of us did in our past we didn't really conclude to be sinful at all. Sometimes we looked upon our actions as simply methods of survival or necessary earthly fulfillments. It was just normal human behavior.

At times we knew some of the things we did had painful consequences but in our spiritually depraved condition we really didn't understand that our behavior was self-destructive. As long as the action appeased a physical, emotional, mental, social or financial need we were happy. We sometimes felt justified in our humanness as long as our actions resulted in a good feeling and produced some immediate, euphoric pleasure. How can it be wrong when it feels right? How can it be bad when it feels good? Although sometimes we know better in our minds and within the depths of our conscience, human desire gets in the way. Human desire overrules our conscience and the thoughts in our heads eventually prove not to be the best choice to make.

You see, before we came to Christ we didn't have the power to freely obey God by doing the things He said would be beneficial to our well-being. As beings subject to a fallen nature, how could we resist the things that would eventually prove to be harmful to us? We were prisoners of the enemy's influence, bound by sin's attraction and held captive by the cravings of our own body. If we think about the old person that some of us used to be, we might agree we were deceived, depraved and disappointed by many circumstances that were beyond our control. The great good news is we serve a God who is in control!

In the midst of our disappointments, unhealthy relationships, daily life challenges and financial stress, our Father continues to love us unconditionally and always will. He will not desert or abandon us. He will never change His mind about how He feels about us just because we made a mistake. Nor will He ever withdraw His love from us because of our imperfections.

There is hope for change. There is hope for transformation. There is hope for deliverance. The enemy comes to kill, steal and destroy. But Jesus has come to restore, give and create. Praise God our Father for His abundant mercy, astounding grace and spectacular love! He loved us so much that He gave us a precious gift: His Son. He sent Jesus to save our lives. What an incredible sacrifice He made, so you and I could be free *(John 3:16-17)*. God's love is amazing, abundant, deep and never-ending. No matter what you and I have done He releases us from the heavy weight of sin. He frees us from agonizing guilt and tormenting shame. Thank God for forgiving our sins and giving us another chance *(Hebrews 10:17, Jeremiah 31:34b)*. What a muddy mess we were! Praise God for cleaning us up *(Ezekiel 36:25-27)*.

Once the Lord cleans us up He empowers us to live a new life. He makes it possible to refrain from certain behaviors while living a Christ-centered life. Abstinence may not be very popular among society, but it is still popular with God. Not only is it popular, but possible with God. We can celebrate abstinence with a joyful heart and a hopeful mindset while living a freedom-filled life.

If you are reading this and you are married and did not practice abstinence before marrying your spouse, there is no condemnation to you. Ask the Lord for forgiveness and keep moving forward. God loves you. He has forgiven and cleansed you. Living a single life is quite a challenge. Trust me I have had my share of challenges. Sometimes I overcame them and sometimes they overcame me. I completely understand. What happened in the past is in the past. God can now use your union as a good example to other couples as long as you have a healthy union. There is now no condemnation to those who are in Christ Jesus. Everything we have done in the past is at the foot of the cross; washed by the cleansing blood of Jesus. Rejoice! Shout Hallelujah!

Now I have to be really honest. There were times I didn't fee joyful, hopeful or free. Is there anybody else in the same boat with me? We are not always on the mountain top. Sometimes we are in the valley. I can recall several times I was elated to be single! I was content not to have to deal with marital issues. It was just me and the Lord and I felt really good about that. I shouted hallelujah with tears of joy thanking God for my precious singleness. Then again I can also recall times when I was discouraged because I didn't have a spouse so I could experience marital bliss. I was crying tears of sadness and asking God, "When Lord when?" I soon discovered having these challenges was just part of the growth process. We are in an ongoing battle so these challenges can be expected *(Galatians 5:20- 26)*. Presently I am elated and celebrating my singleness!

In our wait for a mate, the problem is not in encountering discouragement but the problem is in staying in a place of discouragement. Staying there can open the door for the enemy to come in and entice us out of a place of freedom and lure us back into a place of confinement, bondage and captivity. There were times I received encouragement from a friend. There were other times I had to do like David and encourage myself and talk to my soul. Psalm 43:5 says, "Why so downcast oh my soul? Put your trust in God." Sometimes it was in my moments of discouragement that I made some unhealthy choices regarding relationships but when my soul was encouraged I made much better choices.

Through verbal confession, repentance and trusting by faith in the righteousness of Jesus we can learn to make different choices. We have been released from the authority of the enemy. What a blessing! We are in the arms of a powerful, loving and caring God. What a cause for celebration! We are now free to submit to God's authority and yield to the power of the Holy Spirit. It's a constant challenge but it is possible. It's an ongoing battle but it is possible to live for Christ and feel good about it. All spiritual successes and victories are possible with God! He is our help, our joy and our hope. Apart from Him we can do nothing.

You and I can find joy in Christ, have hope through Christ and experience freedom by the power of Christ. Once this takes place, we can find joy in living the single life. You and I can find joy in living a life of sexual purity. We can be hopeful about one day entering into a marital agreement with someone who is compatible and can help us accomplish God's purpose for our lives. We are free from the "Goliaths" of discouragement and weariness. We are free from making unhealthy choices. There is no condemnation for the mistakes we have made in the past. Our heavenly Father forgives us and throws our mistakes into the sea of forgetfulness. We don't have to allow guilt, shame and regret to overwhelm our minds anymore. Indeed the Lord has truly freed the prisoners!

In order to embrace our new found freedom it is crucial that we cherish our new identity in Christ. As new spiritual creations it is imperative that we understand who we are in Christ and whose we are. We must treasure what we have as a result of who we are. We should also recognize what we can do based on what we now have through Jesus, our glorious Savior.

✦ NUGGET OF WISDOM
We are all in the same boat, rowing with different oars.

Chapter Two
-WHO WE ARE IN CHRIST-

IDENTITY – THE QUALITY or condition of being the same as something or someone else based on a set of characteristics that are associated with origin or nature.

We take on a new identity in Christ with a new quality of characteristics that connect us with the nature of our Maker. Our identity is not restricted to our marital status. In the eyes of God, whether single or married, our value and worth is priceless. I personally believe that singleness and marriage have more to do with *what* we are than *who* we are. They are roles we function in. Whether or not we have a spouse does not define us. We are so much more than our marital status!

When two people get married they become one. Before a person gets married he/she is already one. God honors oneness. Neither status defines our worth, purpose or value as a person. These things are determined by the fact we are all created in God's image and likeness *(Genesis 1:27)*. All beings have valuable worth and purpose whether married or unmarried. The problem is this: some of us have not yet tapped into our worth and purpose. As long as you have breath in your lungs and life in your body it's not too late to tap in!

Unmarried individuals have a unique role to fulfill as well as married persons *(I Corinthians 7:32-40)*. It is not more blessed to be married. It is not more blessed to be single. It is just different. Each status comes with a plethora of bliss and its own set of challenges. One role is not superior or inferior to the other. We are made to feel this way at times but it is simply not true. God has an incredible purpose for all of our lives with or without a spouse. It is very important to embrace this concept. If we don't we may find ourselves spiraling downward emotionally and mentally to a very unpleasant place. Loneliness, frustration and disappointment can continue to overwhelm our minds and rob us of joy and hope that Jesus sacrificed His precious life to give us.

His sacrificial life also gave us freedom. He who the Son sets free is free indeed without a doubt! Not only are we free from eternal damnation through Christ's sacrifice but we are also free from the weight of these emotional burdens. The weight of loneliness hurts. The weight of frustration hurts. The weight of disappointment that results from yet another relationship gone wrong hurts. You and I do not have to allow these emotional burdens to suppress us any longer. Greater is Christ who makes His home in us! We are free to experience joy over loneliness, peace over frustration and hope over disappointment. Why? We can do this because Christ infuses us with inner strength to do all things! Apart from Him we can do nothing worthwhile, but with Him we can soar with wings like eagles!

We are no longer condemned sinners, but redeemed children. God no longer sees the sinfulness of Adam when He looks at us, He sees the righteousness of Jesus. In the natural, although we are still undergoing a continuous transformation, an immediate change has already taken place spiritually. Certain aspects of our existence have been redefined, because we are different people now; not necessarily in our physical appearance, but in our "internal spiritual appearance." Our Father tells us that we are chosen ministers of righteousness, wonderfully made vessels and royal priests. Of course the list goes on and on. Daddy's love letter to us is filled with numerous affirmations that describe who we are in Christ. While I will only expound on a few, it is a potentially empowering exercise to research the many benefits of our identity in Christ. Here are the three that will be discussed in this chapter. We are new creations, spiritual temples and God's masterpieces.

NEW CREATIONS - II Corinthians 5:17

Therefore if anyone is in Christ he is a new creation; old things have passed away, behold all things have become new. (NKJV) Therefore if any person is [in grafted] in Christ (the Messiah) he is a new creation (a new creation altogether) the old [previous moral and spiritual condition] has passed away. Behold the fresh and new has come! (AMP).

This means that anyone who belongs to Christ has become a new person. The old life is gone: a new life has begun! (NLT).

Our new spiritual condition is the key to an attitude of joy, a single season of hope and a life of freedom. It is through Christ that we take on a new nature. It is through the born-again experience that the Lord truly frees the prisoners. Perhaps we should look at where we came from in order to embrace where we are now. We can discover our origin when we refer back to the Garden of Eden in chapter two verses 18 through 25 of the book of Genesis.

Our predecessors, Adam and Eve, were creations of God. God formed Adam from the dust of the ground and fashioned Eve from a rib taken from Adam's side while he was in a deep sleep. There wasn't any surgical procedure done by human hands. No umbilical cord to cut. No stretch marks to distort the skin texture. No nine month incubation period for a fetus to grow. No entry into the world through the birth canal. Adam and Eve were not products of a sexual union, fleshly efforts, or human interference. They were creations of our Almighty God! He is the one who established their earthly existence. He caused them to be living souls by breathing Himself into Adam's lifeless body. Their physical creation was the complete work of God just as our spiritual re-creation through Christ is the complete work of God. In essence our Maker breathed Himself into us as well. The whole human race was in Adam from the very beginning. God is the one responsible for giving us the precious gift of life. What a majestic Creator we worship and serve!

Genesis is the book of beginnings and here is where we see the beginning of singleness. Adam was single enjoying a committed harmonious oneness with His Maker before Eve ever came on the scene. Adam was formed first because it was just part of God's design for the male to be the head in the hierarchy of the family structure. In His singleness Adam learned how to commune with God and have ongoing fellowship with Him. He learned the importance of communication, fellowship, oneness, unity and friendship. Adam also learned the importance of completing a task (naming the animals) and how to work to take care of something entrusted to his care (the Garden of Eden). He even learned the relevance of spending time with someone he loved to better understand their heart (his Creator). Adam learned some valuable relationship tools during his "cool of the day" experiences with the Lord. Likewise, it is in our relationship with the Lord we learn some wonderful tools that can help us in our earthly connections with humans.

We learn the art of effective communication (listening and sharing thoughts). Listening helps us to understand the other person's heart and to receive insight into their likes and dislikes. Sharing thoughts helps us to build trust and unity. Fellowship encourages hope and joy while maintaining a thread of oneness. Spending time with someone we love builds confidence and security. All of these aspects are part of our union with the Lord and with each other. They increase love and strengthen the foundation of any interpersonal connection. These relevant concepts are intrinsic to the thriving survival of any healthy relationship including a marital union.

Could it be that God, in His infinite incredible wisdom, was enjoying fellowship with Adam in the cool of the day while simultaneously preparing him for marital fellowship with Eve? Could it be that the Lord is also preparing some of us for marital fellowship while we enjoy one-on-one talks with Him? If our communication with the Lord isn't good then how can it be in a romantic relationship with a human? Hmm...just a little morsel of spiritual food to chew on.

Adam and Eve were the beginning of us. Just as with them, the new creations we have become are not the result of a sexual union, fleshly efforts or human interference. The new creation experience is the complete work of our awesome God. He formed us by His Spirit and fashioned us by His immense power! Although the image of God that humanity was originally created in was tarnished by the muddiness of sin, now, through the sacrifice of the Son, the Father's image is being restored! Hallelujah!

The Word of God washes us clean as we are beautified (is that a word?) by the transforming power of the Holy Spirit. So what does all of this mean anyway? What this means is we are now able to live morally enriching lives in accordance with our heavenly Father's protective blueprint! With His help we can do it!

- You and I *can* have an attitude of gratefulness!
- We *can* speak forth language that is becoming!
- We *can* refuse to involve ourselves in ungodly relationships!
- We *can* stop talking bad about people outside their presence!
- We *can* resist unhealthy desires!
- We *can* stop procrastinating!
- We *can* gain control over secret addictions!
- We *can* maintain a joyous life of sexual purity!
- We *can* forgive someone who has hurt us!
- We *can* exhibit self-control over our anger and mouth!
- We *can* choose to overcome same gender attractions!

- We *can* turn ungodly habits into Christ-centered routines!
- We *can* make healthier life-style choices!
- We *can* see the value in people who are not like us!
- We *can* make a fair judgment about a situation (or person) after hearing both sides!
- We *can* stop complaining about our lives!
- We *can* be thankful!

The old sinful condition is no longer in control. We have been ingrafted in Christ and are now able to make choices that are acceptable to our heavenly Father! The old way of doing things has passed away. Our spirit has been regenerated. We are new creations. We are born-again. Behold, a fresh new life has begun!

GOD'S MASTERPIECES - Ephesians 2:10

In addition to being new creations we are also God's masterpieces:

For we are His workmanship, created in Christ Jesus for good works, which God prepared beforehand that we should walk in them. (NKJV)

For we are God's [own] handiwork (His workmanship) recreated in Christ Jesus [born anew] that we may do those good works which God predestined (planned beforehand) for us [taking paths which He prepared ahead of time] that we should walk in them [living the good life which He prearranged and made ready for us to live]. (AMP)

For we are God's masterpiece. He has created us anew in Christ Jesus so we can do the good things He planned for us long ago. (NLT)

You and I are His own handiwork; fearfully and wonderfully made. We are divinely inspired works of art. We have been sculpted according to His delicate specifications and uniquely crafted for His good pleasure. Of all the wonderful things God created, we are His greatest "piece." We are His only specimens created in His image and made in His likeness. He re-created us in Christ Jesus so we could do the things He has called us to do beforehand. We can live the godly life He prearranged and made ready for us to live. Will it be easy? No. Can we do it on our own? No way. We need God's Spirit. Now that I'm saved does this mean I won't ever sin again? Of course not. At times we may act out of character. We will make mistakes. Sometimes we will do the opposite of what God says to do. This is all part of the maturation process. Yes God is a righteous judge and sin will be judged but He is also forgiving and patient. Will change happen immediately? Not necessarily. Some change may be immediate but for the most part change is progressive. It is a day by day, week by week, month by month, year by year process. Don't beat yourself up because you made a choice that was not a good one. We live and we learn; we learn and we grow. Living a Christ-centered life is a progressive, continuous process. As we mature spiritually, we should see some noticeable change in our way of thinking, way of living, attitude and conversation.

Here is the spiritual truth: By the power of Christ's crucifixion, we are delivered from the controlling power of sin.

Here is the earthly reality: By the Holy Spirit's power, we must now live out the deliverance that took place on the cross.

With the help of God's Spirit we can maintain a style of life that is pleasing to our Maker. We are free from constantly giving in to unhealthy habits. We are free from having a poor image of ourselves. You are not a hopeless statistic. You are not "good for nothing." You are not who society says you are. You are who God says you are. You are God's workmanship! You are skilled and talented! You are gifted and needed! You have a purpose! You have wisdom! You have potential and the ability to achieve! You are a valuable treasure of significant worth! You are a useful asset! You are special! You are unique! You are priceless! Replace the "you" with "I am" and repeat these words over and over again to increase your sense of worth based on who you are in Christ.

YOU ARE A MASTERPIECE! God's priceless masterpiece.

Spiritual Temples - I Corinthians 6:19-20

Not only are we His new creations and masterpieces, but we are also His Spiritual temples:

Do you not know that your body is the temple of the Holy Spirit who is in you, whom you have from God and you are not your own? For you were bought with a price; therefore glorify God in your body and in your spirit which are God's. (NKJV)

Do you not know that your body is the temple (the very sanctuary) of the Holy Spirit who lives within you, whom you have received [as a gift] from God? You are not your own. You were bought with a price [purchased with preciousness and paid for, made his own]. So then honor God and bring glory to him in your body. (AMP)

Don't you realize that your body is the temple of the Holy Spirit, who lives in you and was given to you by God? You do not belong to yourself; for God bought you with a high price. So you must honor God with your body. (NLT)

In Old Testament times the temple building was an intricate part of the worship of Jehovah. It was a place of sacrifice, worship and reverence unto our Creator God. The temple was set apart exclusively to honor God; its main purpose was to serve as a dwelling place where God would meet His people. God appointed gatekeepers to guard the entrances and maintain the security of the sanctuary. The temple was a place to be respected, undefiled and dedicated unto the Lord for His glory.

In the New Testament the temple is still an intricate part of divine worship. Only in Christ, the temple is not a literal building made by human hands but a spiritual edifice re-created by God. We are His dwelling place now. We are His individual temples as well as His collective temple (which I will expound on a little more later).

Our bodies are individual sanctuaries housing the very Spirit of our Lord. Wherever we go He is right there with us. How can we escape His presence? We are a spiritual house. We are consecrated vessels. Some of our practices must be modified so our lifestyle lines up with our new identity. It's a progressive learning process to go from "It's your thang do what you wanna do" to "In all that you do, do it as unto the Lord."

You and I are set apart for divine purposes. We stand in the prestigious place of a gatekeeper to guard God's precious spiritual house. We have been given the honor of guarding the entrances (heart, eyes, ears, mouth and private areas) for the sake of preserving the sanctity of God's magnificent abode. Our bodies are to be respected, undefiled, and dedicated unto the Lord for His glory. Your wonderful body is the place where the Holy Spirit dwells. My body is the place where the Holy Spirit dwells. He takes up permanent residence inside of us yet exists outside of us at the same time. What an incredible revelation of His presence! We should be mindful of what we do with these wonderful bodies and what we put on the beautiful skin we have been given. It is our reasonable action of worship *(Romans 12:1-2)*. So let us be mindful to honor God with our wonderful body parts. In doing so, we will bring glory to His excellent name.

COLLECTIVE TEMPLE - I Corinthians 3:16

Do you not discern and understand that you [the whole church) are God's temple [His sanctuary] and that God's Spirit has His permanent dwelling in you [to be at home in you, collectively as a church and also individually]? (AMP)

Not only is each believer an individual temple dedicated unto the Lord but we as a whole are a collective temple as a local church. God sees us as a unified assembly joined together in harmony by the blood of Jesus. We are a blood related spiritual family. Although we all know there is no local assembly on this earth that is perfect (because people are not perfect) we are still a family. We are not error free but in the midst of our mistakes we are striving to be Christ-like with His help. I am your sister and you are my spiritual siblings. You may be my sister and my brother from another mother but we still have the same heavenly Father.

We find joy in our relationship with the Lord, AND we can find joy in our relationships with each other. We need each other. I know some of us don't acknowledge that we need anybody but we really do. Now needing each other does not mean we allow people to take advantage of us or that we develop an unhealthy dependency on humans. People must never take the place of God in our lives. People can sometimes be resources but God is always our source. Needing one another just means that since God's Spirit permanently lives in us collectively as the church we can reach out to help each other in times of need. His Spirit in us allows us to care about one another's welfare. His Spirit allows us to show compassion to assist our spiritual siblings whenever possible *(Acts 2:42-45)*.

One way the world is drawn to God is by the genuine concern we demonstrate in our actions towards one another. It is crucial to maintain a constant awareness that people who do not have a relationship with Jesus are watching how we treat and speak to each other. Within the community of believers "outsiders" should be able to witness the love of God through our interactions with our church family. It is wonderful that we say "I love you" when we greet or depart from each other because some people don't hear these words too often. The verbal expression is really nice but the true power of love is in "doing" not "saying." People know it when we show it. People feel it when we reveal it. Showing and revealing is evident in our actions. Genuine love is also shown in these two ways: **respect** and **protect**. Allow me to elaborate:

Respect – Consideration for the feelings, concerns, rights and the challenges of others. To esteem others in high regard and honor. To show forth admiration and courtesy. Think highly of and treat with value.

Many times the breakdown in our human relationships is the result of a lack of respect. As followers of Christ it is imperative that we exhibit respect for all people, including unbelievers, even if they do not agree with some of our concepts or way of life. We show a good example of Jesus when we respect people who do not acknowledge having a relationship with Him. As the family of God it is important we respect each other. It is important we respect ourselves. It is important we respect God's house and God's pulpit.

When we gather together collectively there is a sense of God's presence in our midst which should cultivate mutual respect. So how do we show respect when we gather together? One way is by how we adorn our wonderful bodies. Listen lovely ladies and gorgeous gentlemen, I know it can be a challenge trying to decide what to buy and wear to church sometimes. I don't think most fashion designers have Christians in mind when they are designing their "vogue pieces." So we have to improvise with our wardrobe. Stylish long blazers, long sweaters and loose shirts to wear over form fitting pants are wise investments. Camisoles, mamilla covers, and tee shirts to wear underneath low-cut blouses and see through tops are also necessary items to add to our wardrobe. Girdles, undergarments, body shapers, biker shorts and good quality leggings to wear underneath certain skirts and dresses are just a few more helpful items to have in our closets.

Whether we are shopping in a department store, online or searching through what we already have in our closet, we should be mindful of our selections. We should use wisdom when dressing these wonderful bodies. So what does respect have to do with what people wear? To answer this question let's re-examine the definition for respect, "consideration for the... challenges of others." Let me start with my spectacular sisters.

God made each one of us special. We are unique in our assortment of color, variety of sizes and diversity of shapes and body types. Whether we are splendidly slender, vivaciously voluptuous or somewhere in the middle, we are some fierce ladies! Especially when we have a special event to attend. When we put on an outfit that complements our fabulous body type, accentuate with a nice pair of heels and style our hair (a little extra doesn't hurt) we are a beautiful sight to see! We are truly spectacular!

Ladies, I understand there are moments when we just want to look attractive and feel good about our appearance. There are certain fabrics like cotton, silk, rayon, lycra and spandex blends that feel really good against the skin. There isn't anything wrong with wanting to feel and look our best but we should keep in mind the challenges that some of our brothers may be having when they see certain female body parts "on display" in the house of prayer.

Please hear me. It is not a woman's fault if a man has lust in his heart. Jesus said lust begins in the heart. James said we are tempted by what is already in us. A woman can be wearing a burlap sack, paper slippers and curlers in her hair and a man will still oogle her provocatively because of what is already in his heart. Lust operating in someone's heart is not our fault, however my spectacular sisters, we don't want to be a tool of temptation. Nor do we want to be an instrument of seduction to distract their focus. We love our male spiritual siblings and we want to show consideration for their challenges, not add to them. They see body parts "on display" everywhere else. On the job, in the street, at the park, in the supermarket, while riding public transportation, at the gas station and on the movie screen.

God's house of prayer should be the one place of refuge where women should not be on "display." If a woman only feels good about herself when she is wearing tight or revealing clothing, this may be a sign of a deeper rooted issue. The Holy Spirit and the Word of God can help. Just talk to Him about any insecurity you may have. He will listen. He loves you and wants to help you maintain all forms of freedom. We want to see our brothers as our brothers. We want to show forth admiration and courtesy. In their weakness we should want to be strength to them. As a blood related family we want to help our valiant brothers not hinder them. Spectacular sisters should esteem their spiritual brothers in high regard and honor.

As for my brilliant brothers, please be mindful of your attire as well. Muscle tops, fitted shirts and pants may be comfortable to wear but could present a challenge to some of your spectacular sisters. It's important to think highly of them and treat them with value. Of course if another brother is struggling with same gender attractions that could present a challenge for your brother as well. As adults we can buy and wear whatever we choose but the attire may not be in the best interest of our other family members *(Romans 14, I Corinthians 6:12)*. Just because we can wear what we want doesn't mean it is wise to wear it. As a mature family we can show the world that we respect God, His House, ourselves and each other. We esteem and honor each other in how we clothe ourselves when we come out collectively to worship our Lord.

Another way we show respect in the house of our Lord is in how we speak to each other. The softness of the tongue breaks the bone *(Proverbs 15:1)*. How we say things to each other can either deter anger or provoke it. An aggressive or condescending tone can stir up unpleasant feelings. Not only should we treat each other the way we want to be treated but we should also speak to one another the way we want to be spoken to. We should be careful how we approach each other and converse. Especially when we have a different viewpoint about a matter. It is possible to have a difference of opinion and yet still maintain an agreeable disposition. For example, instead of saying, "Well I disagree" or, "I don't agree with that" or, "That doesn't make any sense" perhaps we should say, "I have a different perspective" or, "That's an interesting thought" or, "I never saw it like that before" then quickly change the subject. Another option is to politely end the conversation then walk away or hang up the phone. Blessed are the peacemakers for they shall inherit the earth *(Matthew 5)*.

Whether it is a group discussion or a private conversation, most people like to express their point. Many of us want to be heard. There is, however, some etiquette that should be practiced to maintain respect. If we learn to exercise a little patience we can allow people to finish their sentences without cutting them off (this concept is necessary in a marital situation). Interjecting a comment without letting a person complete their thought certainly won't strengthen our relationships. It's not a respectful gesture. As singles we want our conversations to be as attractive as our spiritual and physical appearance. We don't want to deter a potential prospect. Love is not rude *(I Corinthians 13)*. If we let the law of kindness rule in our hearts then the evidence will come out when we speak *(Luke 6:45, Matthew 15:10-20)*.

Protect – To keep from damage, attack, theft or injury. To shield or cover from harm or danger.

The same way biological family members are protective of each other, believers should be protective of their spiritual family members the same way. If an unbeliever (or believer) is talking bad about the church or another believer we shouldn't join forces with the devil with our own negative comments. Even if what is being said has an element of truth to it we should still defend our spiritual siblings and God's house. We shouldn't live in the prison of denial but we shouldn't live in the dungeon of gossip either (both are damaging, especially the latter). We can acknowledge the truth without attacking our sister, brother or the house of God. We should shield each other from damaging words that can cause injury. We shouldn't let someone speak ill of others especially when the person being spoken about is not there to explain themselves. That is not fair. That is not the Spirit of Christ operating. Give a person a chance to explain him or herself. How do you even know if what you are hearing is true? How do you know if what is being said is being exaggerated? Even if there is an element of truth to what we are hearing, is it our place to repeat it? Or should we be praying for the person and their weakness? Especially since we have weaknesses of our own that need prayer. Most of the time people do not have the whole story about a situation but are quick to make judgements and make non-edifying comments *(Matthew 7:1-5).*

You and I should make every effort to hear the other side whenever possible so we can form a reasonable and fair conclusion. We should be careful about letting other individuals dump stuff on us that will contaminate the spirit and poison the mind. You and I don't want to present ourselves as an emotional trash can or a spiritual toilet. We are too anointed for such triviality!

If you have itching ears for juicy details about someone else's personal situation then it would be wise to be honest with God about it and ask for His help to overcome this problem. Some people think it is okay to listen to gossip because they are only listening. One who only lends their ear to gossip is an accomplice just as the person who only drives the getaway car in a bank robbery. We don't have to talk bad about people. We sometimes choose to but we don't have to. I heard a radio preacher say, "What's normal for the world should not be normal for the church." Talking bad about people outside of their presence gets higher ratings on TV and is normal for the world. Using the tongue to speak the power of life instead of the power of death is what is normal for the church. Gossip is a joy stealer. Are we so emotionally damaged that we do not feel good about ourselves unless we are talking bad about another person or "throwing someone under the bus"? Whether it is subtle or blatant, gossip separates friends and divides churches. It breaks down the spiritual family structure and creates tension. It unravels the cord of unity.

Let's not be a coward. If we can't lovingly express our thoughts directly to a person then we shouldn't say anything at all. Let's exercise some self-control and stop "stabbing" each other with our tongue in private conversations. Decide in your heart not to let Satan influence your mouth. Let's strive to stop the gossip.

Gossip hurts. The demonic influences operating behind the scene seek to bring strife, division and distraction. It also seeks to degrade someone's character and/or reputation without having all of the facts. The whole body of Christ is affected by it. Who are we imitating when we talk negatively about someone outside of his or her presence? Jesus? Or the devil?

Eavesdropping and slander fall into the same category as gossip. Eavesdropping is the opposite of "minding one's own business." Listening in on other people's conversations and spying on people to see what they are doing and running to tell someone else what you think you overheard or saw is disrespectful. Sometimes our ears and eyes can wrongly interpret something and cause trouble for others. Let's strive not to be trouble makers, fire starters and drama carriers.

Slander robs the collective temple of unity and peace. It is good to concentrate on minding your own business and get your own life in order *(I Thessalonians 4:11)*. It is wise to focus on minding God's business by striving to spread the gospel that brings joy instead of spreading the gossip that brings discontentment.

If Sally has personal information about Becky's life that others do not have knowledge of then it is not Sally's place to "share" it with other people. If Becky wants people to know then she will tell people when she is ready to reveal it. Protecting each other builds unity and genuine love. Brothers and Sisters should strive to maintain the thread of joy, hope and freedom that we inherited from our Savior. This way the world can smell the fresh scent of Christ on us and not the stale stench of the old nature.

Listen, if you have spoken badly about people outside of their presence there is no condemnation. If you have allowed people to come to you and talk bad about someone else there is great hope for you! Simply admit to it and ask God for forgiveness *(I John 1:8-9)*. Let the Lord cleanse your heart and heal your soul. Very often people who gossip, slander and eavesdrop have very low self- esteem, high levels of insecurity and an unhealthy need for attention. Let the Lord increase your esteem and decrease your level of insecurities. Only He can.

Judging others hurts too. No human being is in a place to judge another person because we all have skeletons in the closet. ALL OF US. In fact some of us have dinosaur bones buried in the backyard! The point is this: we all got some bones buried somewhere because we have all sinned against God *(John 8:7)*. If God were to post a video of your past (or present) on social media for all the world to see, what bones would we discover about you? Let's learn not to be critical of other people's mistakes, struggles, shortcomings and testimonies. Let's not be self- righteous. Have compassion for each other. *(I John 3:17)*. Pray for each other *(James 5:16)*. Help each other *(I John 3:17)*. But do not judge each other *(Matthew 7:1-5)*.

Identity is of the essence. Knowing who we are is the beginning of living a changed life. We are God's handiwork and His Spirit's permanent dwelling place both individually and collectively. We have become new people harboring a new set of characteristics that connect us to the nature of our Creator. This is who we are. Let's celebrate! This profound truth enables us to behave and converse in a manner that reflects the beauty of Christ and brings glory to His excellent name. The power of God is within us to respect and protect each other. If we are practicing how to respect and protect each other while we are single then we will be able to do it with a spouse.

God's house is not a playground but holy ground. His pulpit is not a venting box to get back at people. It is a platform to lovingly declare His truth and teach His life- changing principles. The church as a whole is a powerful entity on the earth. Singles are a powerful entity on the earth. Let's celebrate God's house! Let's celebrate singleness! Let's celebrate each other! Let's celebrate Jesus our glorious Savior!

Nugget of Wisdom

You are a masterpiece... not a 'piece' to be mastered.

Chapter Three
-WHAT WE HAVE IN CHRIST-

As a result of being new creations, holy temples and priceless masterpieces there are several helpers in our arsenal. God has given us the Holy Spirit, the Word of God and unlimited access to the throne of God to help us to truly walk in our freedom as born-again believers.

Holy Spirit

But you shall receive power when the Holy Spirit has come upon you. And you will be my witnesses, telling people about me everywhere Acts 1:8 (NLT)

Don't you realize that your body is the temple of the Holy Spirit, who lives in you and was given to you by God? I Corinthians 6:19 (NLT)

I bring you the good news so that I might present you as an acceptable offering to God, made holy (sanctified) by the Holy Spirit. Romans 15:16b (NLT)

The One who created us and separated the waters from dry land; established the laws of physics, gravity and morality; controls weather and celestial elements and; forgives confessed sins; has given us His spirit. There is no way we can live the hope-filled life of a new creation without the Holy Spirit. We are not likely to live a productive Christ-focused single life without the Holy Spirit. The only reason we are able to successfully live in the freedom that Christ has purchased for us is because we have the help we need inside of us. The Holy Spirit isn't really a "what" but a "who." Isn't it good to be reminded of who we have in us?

The Holy Spirit gives power to be effective witnesses for Christ. Part of being an effective witness involves how we live as single individuals. To be a true witness for Christ includes more than just speaking the gospel. We must also live the gospel, telling its truth with our mouths and showing its virtue in our everyday lives. After all, didn't Jesus do both? He spoke the gospel truth to others and lived the gospel truth as an example. The same Holy Spirit who empowered Jesus empowers us as well. We cannot sanctify ourselves. It's simply impossible to live the kind of life the Bible admonishes us to live on our own. We need help. Apart from the Holy Spirit we cannot: be effective witnesses, honor these bodies as God's humble abode, be set apart to sexual purity, or exhibit a joyous attitude. If it were possible to do these things on our own, there would not have been a need for a voluntary crucifixion, resurrection and ascension.

Also, there would not have been a need for Jesus to show us how to live. He is our best example of a single person living a fruitful life. Jesus attended a wedding, took a boating trip, dined with friends, visited people's homes, spent quality time with the "unmentionables" of society, ministered to hurting people, took care of his mother and set aside quality time for prayer. He also shared the gospel message of hope and miraculously fed over 5,000 hungry people. Jesus lived quite a productive life as a single individual. We can learn many good things from His life. One thing that stands out is that no matter what He did, where He went or who was around Him, His mind stayed focused on fulfilling His purpose while instilling hope in others. What a precious lesson for all of us to learn!

As unmarried individuals we can model our lives after His. Now that doesn't mean we have to be serious and deep all of the time. No condemnation to those who are, however, we are allowed recreational time to enjoy ourselves. We all need a recreational activity to help maintain mental, emotional and spiritual stability. If we don't we may run the risk of reaching an unpleasant place called "burnout." Burnout is when we feel overwhelmed because we are handling too many things at once without taking a break. Breaks are important. We need leisure time, vacations and recreational activities to sustain internal equilibrium. These are essential in order to promote a well-balanced life. We should still be mindful of our public behavior, open conversations and private discussions about other people during our time of leisure. The Holy Spirit is still in us when we are on vacation. We should be careful not to grieve (sadden, offend) or quench (ignore, disregard) Him.

We should always be mindful of our purpose. We should be mindful of who we represent even in our fun time. We are believers all of the time wherever we go. We do not take a break from being a believer. I don't think it would be in our best interest to adapt the mindset "anything goes" because we are "off the spiritual clock." Just because the pastor and our church family are not around doesn't mean we should purposely behave in a manner that is unbecoming. God is still around and always watching even when people are not (Hebrews 4:13).

It is okay if we make mistakes. Trust me I've made my share of mistakes. We all have. None of us are in a position to judge or criticize others because we all have a dark past. We are all in the same boat just rowing with different oars. We are not error free. When I say mistakes are okay I mean we don't have to allow condemnation, regret, and guilt to overwhelm us if we have a moment when we are not "behaving" like a Christian. There will be times a button gets pushed and we act out of character. Considering the struggle with our inner nature these moments are to be expected *(Galatians 5:22-24)*. In the midst of our growing process, however, we should be quick to ask God for forgiveness when we have these "out of Christ character" moments. We should also be prepared to apologize if need be. The mistakes we make are just reminders that we need help to live the life Christ intended.

Jesus sent the Holy Spirit to help us. We have the Holy Spirit because we need Him to live a purpose-filled single life. We have Him living in us to help us overcome the challenges of singleness. We need Him to sanctify our character, modify our behavior, cleanse our hearts, purify our mouths and ultimately transform our lives. How can we behave godly, think godly, talk godly and live godly apart from God's Spirit? How can we overcome the inclinations of our self-centered nature without God's power? If we do what we think is right in our own eyes how can we live a life that is pleasing in God's eyes? You and I have God's Spirit living inside of us to assist us in living a joyous life. We will never be Jesus but we can imitate His attitude, mind-set and way of life. Thank God for the Holy Spirit! No matter how troublesome the inclinations of our inner nature there is hope. We have help. We have the Holy Spirit!

The Word of God

I have hidden your word in my heart that I might not sin against you...Give me understanding and I will obey (your word); I will put your principles into practice with all my heart. Psalm 119:11, 34 (NLT)

Jesus said, "If you abide in my word [hold fast to my teachings and live in accordance with them] you are truly my disciples... and you will know the truth and the truth will set you free." John 8:31, 32 (AMP)

Your Word is a lamp to my feet and a light to my path. Psalm 119:105 (NKJV)

The Holy Spirit and the Word of God work together in unison to help us overcome challenges and maintain balance. We need the word. It is important to have fun but also important to understand that single life is not just about having fun. It is crucial to balance recreational time with Bible time. This is important because we must have enough scripture within us to sustain us when we get hit with temptation. Having a busy social life is not going to help when temptation is ringing the bell and sin is crouching at the door. Our Creator offers a way out to escape the jaws of temptation but we may not be able to find the way out if the word is not hidden in our hearts. If we do not have a strong Biblical foundation we risk getting caught in the trap of sin every time. The enemy roams around like a roaring lion seeking someone to devour *(I Peter 5:8)*. He looks for the weakest one in the group. He is a predator. He is a deceiver. When we choose not to read the word our spiritual reflexes are weakened and we make ourselves an easy target. The mind is undergoing a renewal process. There is power in the scriptures but if we are not familiar with the Word how can we pray effectively? We become "prey" when we don't "pray" the Word.

Listen, I understand some of you are saying, "I just don't have time to sit down and read the Bible." I get it. We all have responsibilities. Some of us have quite a schedule. Here are some suggestions. If your budget allows it, you can invest in some Bible CDs. You can pop one in your CD player at home or in the car. This way you can listen to the scriptures while washing dishes, combing your hair, cooking or driving. I have the entire New Testament on CD. Another alternative is to download the Bible on your phone through an app. Then you can listen to the scriptures while riding public transportation, waiting in line at the supermarket or post office or walking down the street (just keep the volume low and be mindful of your surroundings). It doesn't matter if you are reading the scriptures or listening to them as long as the truth is saturating your mind and penetrating your heart.

We can learn quite a few things from the word of God to help us. We must hide the Word in our hearts to resist temptation and overcome sinful habits. We certainly do not want to carry bad habits into a marriage. We must understand the Word in order to obey it, abide in the Word to continue a life of freedom and utilize its principles as a guide for living. We hide the word in our heart by setting aside time to read, study, meditate on, listen to and memorize it. This is how we are able to apply it. There is a difference between having the Word in your head and hiding it in your heart. When it's in our head it's just a bunch of information, facts and knowledge which ultimately puffs up and makes one proud. When it is hidden in our heart we are moved with a desire to apply it. We are also moved with a loving conviction to put its principles into everyday practice. There is an intimate connection between the Word and the human heart. Our love for God should motivate us to live in accordance with His precious love letter to us. Jesus said, "If you love me you will keep my commandments."

As we hold fast to the teachings of Jesus and live in accordance with them we will become more familiar with God's truth then we will begin to experience freedom in various areas of our lives. Whether it is gradual or immediate we will see change as a result of applying God's Word. The Bible is a lamp to show us the moral way to go and a light to guide our decision making as we travel along the path of life *(Psalm 119:105)*. We must overcome the temptation to live our lives based on the world's Christless system. Our decisions should reflect the principles found in God's word. In the midst of the myriad of influences, voices and choices surrounding us there is still hope. We have help. We have the Word of God!

Unlimited Access

And Jesus cried again with a loud voice (it is finished) and gave up His spirit. [At that moment] the curtain (veil) of the sanctuary of the temple was torn in two from top to bottom. Matthew 27:50-51 (AMP)

For through Him (Christ) we Have access by one Spirit to the Father. Ephesians 2:18 (NKJV)

So let us come boldly to the throne of our gracious God. There we will receive His mercy, and we will find grace to help us when we need it most. Hebrews 4:16 (NLT)

Some people who have studied the old testament are familiar with the significance of the "torn veil" at the time of Jesus death. The torn veil is the result of Jesus' sacrifice and why we have access to the presence of God. The Old Testament temple was made up of the outer court, inner court, Holy Place and Most Holy Place (or Holy of Holies). A curtain (veil) separated the Holy Place from the most Holy Place. Only the priests were allowed in the Holy Place.

Only the High Priest was allowed in the Most Holy Place once a year to atone for the sins of the people. Only the High Priest was allowed to approach God. Only the High Priest had direct access and could personally experience the magnitude of God's presence. A veil separated sinful people from a holy God. Our sinfulness kept us from experiencing the intense magnitude of His divine presence. But when Jesus gave up His Spirit on the cross the veil that separated us from our Heavenly Father was torn in two! We are now able to approach God on a personal level because Jesus made it possible through His sacrificial death. What great good news! We now have personal access to His presence! We can stand before His "face" confidently and boldly! We do not have to go through a human priest to talk to God. We do not have to confess our sins to a sinful human man. We can go directly to God for ourselves and ask for His forgiveness! Each believer who is trusting in the sin cleansing blood of Jesus to save them has this privilege. Through Christ, our High

Priest, we have direct access to the Father! Not just once a year but every day! Any time! Anywhere! For any reason!

In His presence is full, complete joy that is overflowing. Rejoice in the Lord always and yet again I say rejoice! When we survive yet another disappointing relationship we can rejoice because He will never leave, reject or withdraw His love from us! When we are struggling with loneliness He wraps us in His warm embrace. This is cause to rejoice! When only one salary is coming into the household and rent gets behind He gives us hope. We can rejoice because He will supply all of our needs according to His glorious riches in Christ Jesus! When food is scarce He gives us hope because He will never forsake the righteous or have their seed begging for bread. We can rejoice because He will make a way and open doors that no human can shut. He is our Shepherd and we will not lack any necessity! When discouragement wants to nag at us and gnaw at the core of our soul there is exceeding gladness in His presence! We have unlimited access to God's presence where there is immeasurable joy and sustaining hope!

If we are having a bad day, a messed up life, or a moment when we step out of character, we can talk to Him about it. If we are discouraged, frustrated, lonely or confused we can go directly to Him. If we are struggling with sexual immorality, unforgiveness, a critical tongue, financial stress, pornography or alcohol we can have a talk with our Father. I'm a witness, He is a deliverer for sure! It is no longer necessary for a sinful man to stand in proxy for us to represent us to the Lord. Jesus represents us. The only mediator between humanity and God is Jesus *(I Timothy 2:5)*. We don't have to suffer in silence anymore. We can freely talk to God and bask in His presence. We don't need to make an appointment to speak to Him. We don't have to settle for meeting with the Deacon because He is too busy. We don't have to leave a message and hope He returns our call. We don't have to worry about information we share with Him leaking out to the ears of people with corrupt hearts. Thank you Lord for direct access to you!

What a privilege we have to talk to and hear from God. Who else can really help us get through the tests, trials, temptations and tribulations of life? Life can be stressful. Relationships are challenging. People can be difficult and uncooperative. Circumstances sometimes seem hopeless. Ah...but there is hope! Don't give up, don't give up, DON'T EVER GIVE UP! Stand up. Look up. Cheer up. But don't you dare give up! Be encouraged. There is hope my friend. We have help. We have personal unlimited access to God Himself! SHOUT HALLELUJAH!

Chapter Three: What We Have In Christ

God has given us everything we need to live a productive life as an unmarried individual. The Holy Spirit, the Word of God, and unlimited access are the necessary essentials we have. These essentials are part of our new identity. We are new creations, holy temples and a priceless masterpiece. We have been reminded of who we are and what we have in Christ. Now let us examine what we can do.

Nugget of Wisdom

Stay rooted in Christ; a firmly planted flower.
Be on the lookout every hour.
God's presence is a shield and tower.
Bathe in the Word and take a Holy Spirit shower.
Because the enemy is seeking someone to devour.

Chapter Four
-WHAT WE CAN DO IN CHRIST-

The Bible declares we can do many things as new creations in Christ. I'd like to discuss a few of these things. We can live a joy-filled life. In our singleness, we can be an effective witness to the world that His power to change lives works. His power to heal broken hearts, renew minds and break destructive habits is real! Our lives should be evidence of His power. We don't have to live a style of life that mimics the world's system of how to do things; a system that our Lord delivered us from. We should not date the way the world does. We should not maintain our relationships based on society's views. We should not make choices based on a system that disrespects our Creator. Our Creator is worthy of respect. He rejuvenates our spirit! He replenishes our soul! He energizes our hearts! He refreshes our mind and restores joy to our lives! We have the capability to know, understand, believe, and speak the Word of God over ourselves. We can live the Gospel. It is a constant challenge and a draining fight at times but we can do it! All spiritual successes are possible with

God's power! Our responsibility is to get into agreement with what God says without twisting, amending, or altering His Word. We are new creations, holy temples, and a masterpiece in God's wonderful eyes. We have been given His Spirit, His Word, and unlimited access to His throne. These truths enable us to do certain things. We can live changed lives, we can overcome destructive habits and we can practice self-control.

LIVE A CHANGED LIFE - Philippians 4:13

I can do all things through Christ who strengthens me. (NKJV)

I have strength for all things in Christ who empowers me [I am ready for anything and equal to anything through Him who infuses inner strength into me. I am self-sufficient in Christ's sufficiency]. (AMP)

Very often people, including myself, have quoted this scripture when faced with a challenging task that had nothing to do with spiritual things. If we lacked energy to do a house chore, had an exam to study for, a driving lesson to take, files at work to organize, a long road trip to take, or whatever, some of us quoted this scripture. The idea was to encourage ourselves to complete a task that we really did not feel up to doing. For the most part using this scripture in such circumstances is not inherently bad, but allow me to challenge you to see this scripture from a very different perspective.

In its context, this verse was an admonition from Paul that we can be content in whatever situation we find ourselves in when we depend on the strength of Christ and not our own human strength. One principle being taught here is that we should depend on Christ's strength to obtain spiritual success and contentment. Christ infuses us with strength on the inside to empower us to resist giving into unfavorable patterns of behavior. We can stop talking bad about people outside of their presence because Christ gives us strength to overcome the perils of our mouth. We can stop complaining and finding fault with others. We can practice sexual purity because Christ empowers us to master those urges until we are married. His power really does work! I am a living witness that it does! We can lose our desire to watch pornography and other inappropriate movies. We can live sin-conquering lives because Christ infuses us with inner strength. We can be an effective witness for Jesus who enables us to live a changed life.

Overcoming Destructive Habits - Mark 10:27

Humanly speaking, it is impossible. But not with God. Everything is possible with God. (NLT)

Kept within its context this scripture refers to the salvation of a rich man whose possessions are the center of his heart, the priority of his life and the means of his dependency. How can such a person obtain salvation? It is a work that is only possible with God. The lesson here is salvation is only possible with God's power. The principle here is all spiritual achievements are accomplished with God's power. It takes more than human will power and simple logic to overcome destructive habits. We need His help and intervention in order to enjoy a conquering life before a spouse comes into our lives.

A habit is a pattern of behavior which is the result of repetitive actions/choices that give insight into a person's character, moral position, and daily way of thinking. Lifestyle is based on repetitive behavior. All sinful behavior falls into the category of destructive habits. They are destructive because they hinder us from having a healthy relationship with God and with people. Destructive habits produce consequences that not only hurt us but sometimes the people around us. Bad habits may be *hard* to break but *not impossible* to break.

It is possible to quit smoking. It is possible to refrain from cursing and using profane words to express ourselves. It is possible to stop making the same toxic relationship choices. It is possible to better budget our finances and give a portion to the House of God. It is possible to find healthy ways to numb the emotional pain and mental anguish we sometimes feel. In many cases the pain and anguish often results from an offense or a childhood issue that was never resolved. It is possible to have a change of heart and not physically and verbally abuse others. It is possible to forgive and let go of grudges. How are all of these things possible? With God's help. There is immeasurable hope in the midst of our many challenges that often damage our interpersonal connections. Yes, all things are possible with God!

Practicing Self-Control - Galatians 5:22-23

But The Holy Spirit produces this kind of fruit in our lives: ...self-control. (NLT)

So prepare your minds for action and exercise self-control. Put all your hope in the gracious salvation that will come to you when Jesus Christ is revealed to the world. So you must live as God's obedient children. Don't slip back into your old ways of living to satisfy your own desires. You didn't know any better then. But now you must be holy in everything you do, just as God who chose you is holy.
I Peter 1:13-15 (NLT)

Self-Control. How can such a small compound word be so immensely challenging for us to practice? How can I control myself when I desire to have something that is not healthy or good for me to have? Good questions. I am glad you asked. (It shows you are paying attention). Allow me to offer an answer:

Notice the scripture says the Holy Spirit produces self-control. In order to maintain discipline over our ungodly desires, urges, habits and cravings we must first recognize that it takes the power and Spirit of God to do so. It is a fruit that must be produced within us. Not only does the Holy Spirit produce self-control but He also helps us to practice it. As we come to know God better and grow in our understanding of living to satisfy God and not ourselves, we will develop self-control. We will be able to think clearly and exercise discipline over our self-focused desires.

Some people say *you just need willpower*. Well quite honestly I think it takes more than will power to resist temptation and overcome non-edifying habits. There is a very big difference between will power and Holy Spirit power. Will power focuses on human strength and our limited ability. Holy Spirit power focuses on God's strength and His unlimited ability. Self-control is the ability to gain and maintain control (authority, dominion) over fleshly urges, desires, habits, choices and cravings. In its simplest form self-control is the ability to say "no" when you really want to say "yes."

I'm not saying it's easy to say "no" to anything. Remember, all things are possible with God, but not all things are easy. Many times you and I can't say "no" until we have learned how to develop the desire to say "no." It's a progressive process. It is a combination of recognizing our need for God and realizing that only the Spirit of God can help us. Whenever we find ourselves slipping, He is there to grab us and pull us up. His grace enables us to overcome guilt, shame and condemnation. A righteous person falls seven times but the Lord always picks Him up. If we confess our faults to Him He is faithful and just to cleanse us from all unrighteousness. Isn't that great good news? With His help we can practice self-control, live a disciplined life and experience a "winning feeling" on a regular basis.

You and I can learn to discipline our mouths. We can learn to control heterosexual desires and same-sex attractions. We can change bad habits and form godly habits. Mastering self is not easy but it is possible with God!

Through Christ, our heavenly Father has redefined who we are and has given us everything we need to live a "free" godly life and have more successful relationships. We are new creations, spiritual temples and priceless masterpieces. We have the Holy Spirit, the Word of God, spiritual authority and unlimited access to the throne of God. With this new-birth empowerment, we can live changed lives, overcome destructive habits and practice self-control. For those who want to. Of course living this kind of life does come with its challenges. It would be great if the process were as smooth as it sounds. Maturity does not happen overnight. We have to be patient with ourselves and with others. Obstacles will always arise to try to hinder us. So now, in the next chapter, let's examine some of the obstacles that often cause us to stumble. These obstacles often hinder us from living the life God intended for us to live. They also interfere with our interpersonal connections with one another.

A Selah Moment: Self-reflection Thoughts
- What area in your life do you have self-control?
- What area do you lack self-control?
- Have you talked to God about the bad habits you need to get rid of?
- Are you cooperating with the Holy Spirit to produce change? Or are you quenching Him and resisting His help?

NUGGET OF WISDOM
You can't get rescued from drowning
if you keep fighting the lifeguard.

Part II

Looking Back At The Prison Door: Reasons We Go Back

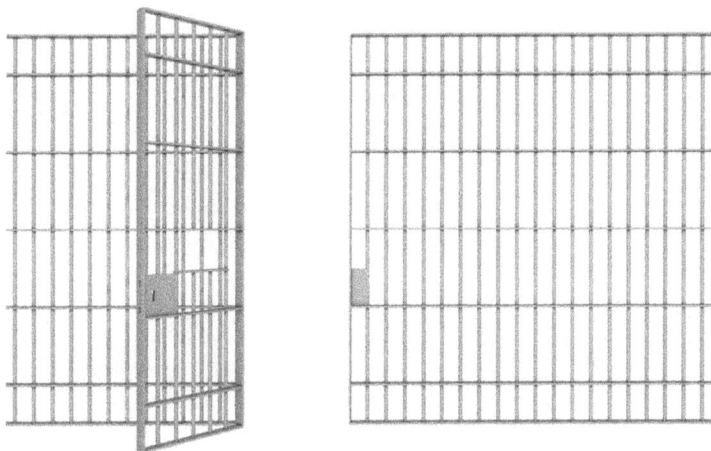

CHAPTER FIVE
-BREAKING BONDAGE -

Do not be entangled again with a yoke of bondage
Galatians 5:1

Before we discuss the obstacles that often hinder us or entangle us again, let's discuss reasons to rejoice as unmarried individuals. We have reasons to celebrate our blessed singleness! This is our time to get to learn God and better understand ourselves before we get into a romantic relationship where we will have to learn to understand someone else. Many times we want "just the right" person but we need to make sure we are "just the right" person for someone else. This is our time to focus on ministry and help others in need. During our single season we can work on becoming a mature, emotionally healthy individual so we don't "abandon ship" too soon because of unresolved personal issues.

Now, if you are single due to divorce there is no condemnation to you. Sometimes relationships just don't turn out well no matter how hard we try to make it work. When we take responsibility for our part in the break up, God waits with open arms to forgive, heal and restore. He gives direction on how to overcome our personal challenges within ourselves. We must refrain from pointing a finger of blame and examine the person in the mirror. We cannot change others but we can certainly work on changing ourselves. The idea is to become more like our amazing Savior. In order to do so we must be willing to make adjustments to our character. We must also acknowledge any hurt we have caused the other person during the union. When we come to God with a heart of repentance asking for forgiveness, He hears and forgives. All is forgiven at the cross of Christ.

Perhaps you thought it best to leave the marriage because you just couldn't take it anymore...whatever the "it" was. Listen, whatever happened to cause the union to dissolve is in the past now. You must learn from the situation and move forward.

Perhaps the divorce was not your preference. Maybe you wanted to salvage the marriage but the other person is the one who wanted to leave the relationship. Sometimes we have to bear the consequence of someone else's decision. Talk to the Lord about how the whole experience has affected you.

Let Him help you so your mind can be healed and your heart can be free of any anger, hurt or vengeful feelings you may be wrestling with.

If your singleness results from becoming a widow or widower, I pray the Lord continues to comfort your heart. You may need to speak to a Christian grief counselor to help you through your grieving process. The Lord is with you in your aloneness as you readjust to single-hood all over again. The Lord loved you through your loved one while he/she was here with us. Now is an amazing opportunity to allow the Lord to love you through His Spirit. If you are relieved because your marriage was not a healthy union then allow the Lord to heal you so you can be an emotionally healthy individual.

During the single days it's a great idea to get to understand yourself. Reflect:

- What brings you down or causes discouragement?
- What excites or motivates you?
- Are you argumentative?
- Do you yell or scream to make your point?
- Is it your way or no way?
- What angers you?
- How do you usually deal with anger?
- What calms you down?

- Do you struggle with laziness and procrastination?
- Are you consistently late?
- Does your tardiness affect other people?
- How about anxiety, worry and impatience?
- Do you overthink things?
- Do you underthink things?
- Are you willing to cooperate with someone else's way of doing things?
- How are you at managing money and receipts?
- Are you wrestling with self-centeredness?
- Can you be trusted?
- Or are you dishonest in your dealings with people?
- Do you struggle with telling the truth?
- Does every conversation have to center around you and your world?
- Are you a person who sometimes interrupts people when they are speaking?
- Are you a gossiper?
- Do you talk too much about things that are none of your business?
- Do you have problems sharing your money or time?
- Are you a good communicator?
- Or do you struggle to communicate how you feel?
- How about unforgiveness from a previous relationship?
- Can you admit when you are wrong and accept responsibility when you offend or hurt someone?
- Do you covet other people's mates?

- Are you flirtatious because of a need for validation and to feel attractive?
- Do you struggle with jealousy or vindictiveness?
- Do you speak with mean words or a harsh tone?

You see, marriage involves being able to forgive your spouse from time to time. You will offend each other sometimes whether purposely or unintentionally. Marriage also involves being able to apologize to your spouse at times and admit when you are wrong. In fact there are times you may need to apologize even when you are not wrong. Hmm.

As a single person, if you have problems apologizing, letting things go, admitting when you have made a mistake or sharing your space and resources then marriage may be a very difficult and unpleasant experience for you...and for the other person as well. Denial is another issue that can contribute to an unpleasant marital experience. It's like fumbling around in the dark with shades on - complete darkness. How can you get the help you need if you are not willing to admit you have an issue? These are just some of the things we need to understand about ourselves BEFORE we commit to a marriage. Sometimes people do not like to be alone with themselves. Perhaps this is because society has attached such a negative stigma to being by yourself. Single-hood is a time to get to know yourself. It's okay to be alone sometimes but it is never okay to be isolated. The devil meets us in isolation (long-term separation from people). God meets us in aloneness (momentary separation from people). We can learn from Jesus' single lifestyle. He spent quality time with other people but He also spent quality time away from other people...alone... with God. Jesus is always our best example to follow.

There are also some good practical reasons to celebrate our blessed singleness. We can spend time discovering our incredible gifts and wonderful talents that our gracious Lord has bestowed upon us! Thank God we don't have to check in with anybody about how long we will be out or when we are coming home! We can pretty much come and go as we please. We don't have to cook or order in if we do not want to! We can have two bowls of our favorite cereal or a peanut butter and jelly sandwich for dinner and nobody is complaining about it! Praise God we can have the whole bed to ourselves! More room to spread out. Less money is spent on household expenses and toiletries! Less laundry to do! Yahoo!

Some of us may not appreciate the advantages of these things (and other celebratory advantages of being single). But if we don't search for the good in the neighborhood of single-hood and change our perspective then we may very likely find ourselves in a place of despair spiraling downward deeper into the depths of disappointment. We may also find ourselves constantly giving in to the woes of loneliness. These are just some of the challenges that can lead to "being entangled again" with unfruitful relationships, unhealthy beliefs, old destructive habits...or all of the above.

"Entangled again with a yoke of bondage" *(Galatians 5:1)* has to do with returning to an old habit or unhealthy belief. We return to the Law: the old way of doing things. It's like wallowing in the mud after you have just taken a shower. It is also like eating vomit that just came out of your mouth *(Proverbs 26:11)*. It is like returning to the jail cell after the warden said, "you are free to go."

Earlier in Chapter One, we talked about how the Lord gives joy, hope and freedom. We read, "The Lord frees the prisoners" *(Psalm 146:7)*. We were once spiritual prisoners but now we are free with the promise of joy and hope. We are now new creations, holy temples and a priceless masterpiece. We have the Spirit of God living inside of us, the Word of God to guide us and unlimited access to God's presence. We can live victorious lives, overcome bad habits and practice self-control over our unbridled desires. We are free...aren't we? So if all of this is true then why do we continue to struggle with unhealthy choices? If we know who we are, what we have and what we can do then why do we have such difficulty resisting temptation? Why do we have such a hard time taming our tongue, managing finances, releasing wrongs done against us and practicing sexual purity? Is it really possible to live a free life? It seems easy to speak, preach, quote, teach, read and sing the Word but why such a challenge to live it?

Let's examine some factors like the internal battle, unmet legitimate needs, temperament and some childhood issues that may contribute to us being entangled again with a yoke of bondage. A yoke of bondage can be symbolic of an unhealthy romantic or platonic relationship. It can also be a form of sexual gratification or a bad habit. A lack of self-control, loneliness and a misunderstanding of how we define love are some other factors. We need a better understanding of what genuine love is and what it isn't. We will also look at some "door openers" that arouse our senses and can make it difficult to resist yielding to unhealthy desires. Let's see if together we can locate where our struggle stems from and why we sometimes go back to the emotional (mental) prison.

Internal Battle

Entangled – caught up in something and unable to free oneself on your own. To get involved in a disturbing or complicated situation from which it is difficult to escape. Ensnared or trapped. Twisted together.

Romans chapter 7 speaks very vividly about the internal battle that every believer faces. Galatians chapter 5 speaks very vividly about the wrestling match going on between the Spirit and the flesh. There are two natures operating through the heart and mind of every born-again believer. We are partakers of God's divine nature yet we also have a human (or sinful) nature within us as well. These two natures each have a different set of goals to accomplish and as a result are at constant war with each other. The Spirit (the power of God within every believer who develops the character of Christ in us) draws us closer to God to do what is godly. The flesh (the inclinations, lusts and desires of our human nature) pulls us away from God to do what is ungodly and destructive to self and to others.

Here is an example: Imagine a saved mother, an unsaved father and their teenage daughter. The father and mother both live in the same house and occupy the same space. The mother is trying to influence the daughter to do what is selfless and godly. The father is trying to get her to do what is selfish and ungodly. The daughter is caught in the middle trying to make a choice based on the two opposing "voices" speaking into her ear. In the same manner, both the Spirit and the flesh live in the same house and occupy the same space (in us). Each one is speaking into our spiritual ear trying to influence us to make a decision based on their influence. Does this make sense? I hope so.

You see, true believers have a genuine desire to do what is right and good. The spirit is always willing but the flesh is always weak. We want to do what is honorable and godly. We want to please God. But there is another force within trying to block us and hinder our intentions. Paul said, "When I want to do good, evil is always present with me. What I want to do...I don't do. What I don't want to do is what I practice. These opposing powers (Spirit and flesh) are probably most intense when we are faced with difficult moral choices or temptations. Many choices we make are the direct result of one of these influences. When we are stressed, frustrated, hurt, annoyed, disrespected, discouraged, impatient, depressed, struggling financially, lonely or sexually aroused, we must be mindful of our decisions. Either the Spirit or the flesh will influence our actions and words. It depends on which one is stronger at the moment. We are most likely to give in to the flesh when our legitimate needs are not being properly met.

Legitimate Needs

We all have a basic need for food, water, shelter and clothing. We also have emotional needs as well. All human beings have a legitimate need to be loved and feel loved. We want to be accepted and secure. When these needs are not met the right way we often seek to meet them in a manner that is not conducive to our well-being. Very often we end up going back to the internal prison because one or all of these needs are not being met. Hebrews 4:16 admonishes us to come boldly before the throne of God where we will find more of His grace to help us in our time of need. Why? Because if we do not come to Him for His help then we will very likely meet the need in a way that will not prove to be beneficial for us.

We are likely to get "twisted together" with something or someone who ultimately becomes the source of our downfall. An unforeseen circumstance such as the loss of employment, death of a loved one or health issue can leave us with a real need. Very often it is in our time of need that we are most challenged by temptation. We will find ourselves giving into something that in the end will prove to be detrimental to our relationship with God, our relationship with others and our relationship with ourselves. This is what temptation is all about. One purpose of temptation is to get us to meet our needs apart from God – without Him or His resources. We are "pulled" to do the opposite of what God says to do. Sometimes our emotional needs based on our temperament can also play a part in this.

Temperament

Temperament has to do with certain characteristics of a person's personality. Some people are defined as Choleric, Sanguine, Melancholy or Phlegmatic. Some of us are a combination of all four. What sets us apart is the temperament that dominates the other three. If you are interested, feel free to do further research on your own. If not, it's okay. No condemnation. There is a special test that must be taken to determine which type you are. This only helps us to better understand ourselves so we can go before the Lord for His help to meet our emotional needs in a healthy manner. Identifying child-hood issues that were never resolved can also help us to better understand ourselves.

Childhood Issues

Many emotional and mental issues we wrestle with in our adult life are a direct result of our childhood experiences. Actions produce results and results lead to an ongoing outcome. For example, a household with a missing parent or absentee father results in feeling inadequate because of a lack of parental affection. The outcome is this: always having a need for masculine/feminine affection or attention. It can also lead to having a need for constant approval from a person in authority.

Here are some other experiences: A parent suddenly decides to leave the family without warning: abandonment. A high school sweetheart ends the relationship to be with someone else: rejection. Someone close to us violates our body against our will: sexual abuse. A caregiver is hardly ever around to take care of our basic needs: neglect. A parent is never physically there for us: absenteeism. A sibling or outsider is preferred over us: favoritism. A dysfunctional classmate wants to call us names or beat us up for fun: bullying. A child grows up in a household of constant lack: financial insecurity. Extreme punishment or irrational methods of discipline: abuse. All of these things contribute to many of the insecurities we wrestle with as adults.

Unresolved insecurities can lead to "being entangled again with a yoke of bondage." Jesus is our hope for joy, restoration and emotional healing from past childhood issues. Call on His name and let Him heal you.

All of these issues threaten our legitimate need for love, acceptance and safety. These insecurities are just some of the childhood experiences that lead to deeper adult issues if left unresolved. Some of the deeper issues include: depression, discouragement, rage, inferiority complex, self-hatred, meanness, apathy, hard-heartedness, hopelessness and suicide. Many times we make unhealthy relationship choices in our adult life because we are still "traumatized" by a childhood incident that left us feeling unloved, unaccepted and unprotected. Vulnerable people often drown themselves in alcohol, drugs, sexual activity, the night club scene, cigarettes, pornography, and toxic relationships as a solution to help cope with these issues. Ahhh...but we do not have to wrestle with feeling unloved, unaccepted and insecure anymore!

God loves us without condition and accepts us graciously

with all our imperfections. He enables us to be secure in Him. He brings healing. Despite what we endured growing up He is still able to pour purpose into us and remind us of our significant value and worth. He embraces us within the warmth of His bosom and hides us beneath His wing!

A lack of self-control and a lack of discipline will always lead us to get "caught up" in something or "twisted together" with someone that God has already delivered us from. Self-control and discipline can be interchangeable in meaning but can also be distinct in definition. I believe self-control is the ability to say "no" to something (or someone) you really want to say yes to. I also believe discipline is being able to be around that "forbidden" thing and not yield to it because you are no longer interested in it. Self-control and discipline are partly about developing a new interest in something else. A new goal must become stronger than the old desire (I will talk more about this in part three).

When we feel unloved, unaccepted, and insecure there is a nagging void for genuine affection and approval. This may mean hooking up with a "bad" boy to do mischievous things, telling a lie to appear more likeable or cuddling up with a naked body who is not God's best for us. We continue our quest for love, acceptance and security...many times throughout our entire adult life. When we can't find a human to fill the emptiness then we may turn to alcohol, food, drugs, pornography, gambling or some other "comfort."

Sex is probably the most popular of all these comforts. There are people who don't drink liquor, use drugs, smoke cigarettes or gamble. But they do have sex. Sex can make one feel loved, accepted and secure. Bear in mind, sometimes, we become entangled again with a yoke of bondage to a relationship, activity or unhealthy habit because we are still trying to feel the love, acceptance and security that we didn't feel growing up. Many vices that plague humanity (especially those of a sexual nature) usually stem from one of these emotional needs that were denied us as a child. Sin is very attractive when we are trying to fill a void, numb the pain inside, escape the past or just feel better about life. Many times these challenges are amplified when one is part of the single community. Let's take a look at one of the main things that we turn to for comfort concerning these emotional needs...sexual gratification.

NUGGET OF WISDOM
It's difficult to find the light switch
in the dark with shades on.

CHAPTER SIX
-SEXUAL GRATIFICATION -

*Flee from sexual immorality. Every sin that a man
does is outside the body but he who commits
sexual immorality sins against his own body.*
I Corinthians 6:15-20

In this chapter we will cover something that is often a challenge for many of us, especially singles who desire to live a life of sexual purity. Of course, intimacy is not the only thing singles are challenged by, but many times it is at the top of the list of challenges. I realize I must tread lightly and be sensitive to people with this very delicate subject. At the same time, I believe it is important to be as honest, open and realistic as possible. With God's help, I will do my best to bring some balance.

Truly my intention is to encourage healing, restoration and freedom from relationships and activities that can prove to be detrimental to us. My prayer is that we would have a better understanding of human intimacy that will challenge us to make healthier decisions during our season of singleness. With that being said, let's see what we can discover.

As I mentioned in chapter five, there are some things we tend to turn to for comfort when we are looking to fill a void. The internal battle, unmet legitimate needs and unresolved childhood issues often lead us to return to the familiarity of past comforts such as sexual intimacy, compromising our joy, hope and freedom. We end up twisted together with someone or caught up in a relationship that can turn into a complicated situation. This can put us right back in the prison that Christ rescued us from. Sexual intimacy is very comforting. But why? What is the big deal anyway? Let's talk about it in greater detail.

Sex. Such a small word with such enormous interest. We see it, hear about it, talk about it and think about it. Advertisers use it to sell products, girls are warned it is the only thing boys are after and recording artists sing about it. Some people become vindictive monsters when they find out the one who they love is getting it from someone else. Sex can be very powerful. Like fire and water, it can be both constructive and destructive to human life. It can be used to influence someone's will, behavior or actions. It can manipulate one's choices by controlling how one thinks, or motivate one to do special favors. It can be a stress reliever too. Certainly, it is the icing on the cake between a man and a woman in a healthy marriage. I personally believe sexual intimacy is one of the deepest, most beautiful expressions of human love that exists. Anything established and instituted by our God is truly beautiful. I think sometimes we get so caught up in the ecstasy of the activity that we lose focus of what is more important in a relationship. I know I did back in the day.

I don't know about you, but I was one of those people who thought sex was equivalent to love. During my tenure as a young adult I didn't know there was a difference. There wasn't anyone to teach me the two were very distinct by definition. It was forbidden to be mentioned in my household growing up so there was no way there would have ever been a candid discussion about it. Much later in life I discovered sex is the result or fruit of love, but it is not love itself. I didn't learn that precious nugget of truth until I came into the family of Christ and my mind was renewed. I have learned that spiritual compatibility, character, friendship, communication, trust and the ability to resolve conflict are very important in a meaningful relationship. Sexual intimacy is difficult to achieve if these elements are missing. Without these intrinsic essentials you may have sex but not true love. It is in my relationship with the Lord that I am learning the true beauty of an intimate relationship without the sexual factor attached.

I believe sex is an action or activity to satisfy a physical desire.

I believe love is a series of actions toward a person to show genuine concern and interest for their well-being combined with a decision to continue with the commitment when challenges arise. Intercourse should confirm a love that is already there.

If you are confusing sex with love, there is hope for you. Now is an amazing opportunity to ask the Lord for forgiveness and for Him to help you to understand the difference between sex and love. Let me also add, no woman is in a position to judge another woman's sexual past, because many of us have one.

Some of us are in a wonderful relationship with the Lord! We belong to Him. We are the sheep of His pasture. We are the apple of His eye and the center of His heart. The only union more intimate than the one between a husband and a wife is our union between us and our heavenly Father. The deepest bonding between a husband and wife is consummated through the intimacy of their sexual experience. The deepest bonding between us and our Father is through the intimacy of our spiritual connection with Him. Because of the closeness we have with Him He gives us access to the most intimate part of himself and develops a strong oneness with us that cannot be compared with any other relationship. We begin to see the world through His eyes and feel the beat of His heart. His desires become our desires. His truth becomes our truth. He is incredibly patient with us and has a high level of tolerance beyond the capacity of any human being. He loves us without condition and gives us thousands of second chances when we mess up. When we are faithless, He remains faithful to us. He doesn't divorce Himself from us. He doesn't cheat on us. He doesn't leave us to raise children without His help. Even if we turn our back to Him, He extends His hand to help us! Every other relationship is incomparable. Anything that interrupts this special harmony is harmful to our glorious fellowship with Him.

If you are not in a relationship with the Lord, then you can be! It is not too late now, but one day it will be. Today is the day of salvation. Do not harden your heart. Jesus is waiting to welcome you with open arms of abundant love! Come to Him! Believe Jesus was crucified on the Cross and raised from the grave to save your soul. Admit you are a sinner and ask for His forgiveness.

Pre-marital Sex/Fornication

Sexual intimacy is one of the deepest, most beautiful expressions of human love that exists. Being physical with someone you believe you have a connection with feels like the most natural thing to do. It may feel good and feel right. After all, when two people feel they have a connection, what better way to express their consensual affection? Makes perfect logical sense, doesn't it? Sure it does. We are able to put the issues of life on pause and feel good in the moment. So then, what is the problem? Sometimes that good feeling can be misleading or can be a smoke screen to a more serious problem. Shouldn't we find comfort in His arms and not in the arms of a person? Will sexual behavior outside of marital covenant strengthen your relationship with Jesus?

You see, there is a reason the marriage bed is undefiled *(Hebrews 13:4)*. God is not trying to stop us from having fun. He only wants to protect our delicate hearts and preserve our precious bodies. Sometimes a physical union with someone can cloud your judgment about that person's character. The physical connection can also cause us to go into denial about the person's inability to manage anger in a healthy manner. This can lead us to sometimes miss red flags. Sometimes we see the warning signs and just ignore them. At times we may offer excuses to try and justify questionable behavior because we are blinded by the pleasure of the physical experience. God with His gracious love and magnificent mercy is just protecting us from being misused, abused and confused. Our Creator does not want us to be treated like an emotional teabag: used until all of the flavor is gone. What do we usually do when all of the flavor is gone out of a teabag? We throw it away and look for another one to use.

In chapter two we discussed who we are in Christ. Keeping this in mind, shouldn't a masterpiece be handled differently because of its immense value and significant worth? As a new creation our views on sexual activity must change when we are drawn to Christ. Should we follow the suggestions of other people who try to advise us on what they think we should do with our temples? There are times when we singles sometimes feel pressured to give in to the flow of the current and just ride the wave. Sometimes family members, friends and even the person we are dating may mean well but please do not let well-meaning people pressure you or push you into participating in things you are not comfortable with. Stand your ground and hold firmly to your convictions. You are not weird. You are unique! You are not holier than thou. You are chosen! You are not a party-pooper. You are a trend setter! There isn't anything wrong with you. You are simply a person with a desire to live an abstinent lifestyle. Perhaps you have sinned against your own body in the past but not anymore. Good for you! God has tossed the past into the sea of forgetfulness and will never remind you of it again. Perhaps you are sinning against your own body now. There is no condemnation to you. Just ask the Lord for forgiveness. Let Him cleanse your heart. Let Him empower you to overcome those desires. He is able to help you put those desires in storage until the appointed time. Allow His love to heal your mind and emotions. You are still a masterpiece!

If you have decided to refrain from sexual activity until marriage, that is a very good decision and is in agreement with God's standard regarding sexual purity. It is important to connect yourself with people who will give you support that lines up with God's Word. Bad advice can corrupt good intentions. Make it a habit to surround yourself with people who will encourage you and cheer you on. Avoid individuals who promote carnal compromise, bring you down about your convictions and make you feel less than. Learn to hear God's voice for yourself through your spirit and through His Word so you do not get caught up making relationship choices based on insecurities, loneliness, lust or someone else's experiences. Humans tend to be unstable in their mannerisms. One week they are shouting "Hosanna!" singing your name with honor. The next week they are shouting "Crucify Him!" cursing your name and forgetting every good thing you have ever done. Isn't that what they did to Jesus? Don't allow yourself to be misled by someone else's relationship experience.

Also, bear in mind, someone else's experience may not necessarily work for you. People like to give the highlights and conveniently leave out the fine print regarding their personal experience. They will conveniently forget to mention how abusive, inconsiderate, disrespectful and unfaithful the person was before he/she saw the light and got it together. How long did they endure the darkness before their significant other finally saw the light? Are you willing to endure that long? How many times did they have to lay in the bed crying painful tears because of emotional neglect or physical rejection? How many times did they have to get in the car and drive around the neighborhood looking to see whose driveway his/her car was parked in front of? This is just some of the fine print. Just because someone else was willing to tolerate certain behaviors does not mean the same will work well for you. Do not feel you need to get involved in a relationship because hearing the highlights of someone else's experience is increasing a desire to be with somebody.

At the end of the day it is about your relationship with God not with other people. Remember, people come and go but God is here to stay! People are inconsistent with their feelings and actions but God is the same yesterday, today and forever! He is consistent and changes not! He will never relinquish His hold on you. He always has your back! He supports you in your decision to refrain from premarital sex. You are not alone. People do not have to have sex; they choose to have sex. It is possible to go from "I choose to have sex because I want to" to "I do not want to have sex anymore outside of marriage because I choose instead to truly honor God with my body." The power of Christ can change our "want to." It is a challenging journey but His power is able to do it! If He freed me, He can free you too! Stay encouraged! Sexual purity may not be popular with some people but it is still popular with God! Aren't His thoughts about you the only ones that really matter?

Self-Pleasure
Giving oneself pleasure may seem very innocent. I mean after

all, nobody's feelings get hurt, nobody gets pregnant and nobody can get an STD from doing it. Seems like the most natural thing to do when there is no one else around to satisfy us during those moments when we feel aroused. Although the scriptures do not directly address this topic it does provide principles for us to govern our actions by. For example, the Bible does not address the use of cocaine or crystal meth but it does give us principles like, "your body is the temple of the Holy Spirit," or "in all that you do, do it as unto the Lord." The principle here is that we should honor God with our body by not polluting it with substances that can damage our mental, emotional, and physical health or shorten our lives. In the same manner, we can apply the principle behind the scripture, "the husband's body belongs to the wife and the body of the wife belongs to the husband." According to the scripture, physical pleasure should be given and received by our spouse, not by ourselves.

Some of you may be thinking, "Well God maybe if you send me a mate I wouldn't have to take care of myself." If this is how you feel I certainly understand. It is a very genuine and valid concern. There isn't anything wrong with you if you feel this way. Maybe, though, there is a really good reason why we should resist the urge to appease ourselves. Could it be, God is trying to teach us to have some self-control before we establish a long term committed relationship with someone? If we can't control our hands and urges when we are not in a committed relationship then how will we be able to do it when we are in one? If we can't say "down girl" or "cool it soldier" when we are alone by ourselves then will we be able to do it when we are involved with someone? How about when you are married and your spouse must go out of town for business for a few days? Or take care of a sickly parent for a couple of months? When the spouse is unavailable will you be able to discipline yourself or will you step outside of the covenant and indulge in an affair? If we can't exercise self- control before we get married then how will we be able to do it after we get married?

Our gracious God has given us some amazing principles to adhere to on our single journey. We all have our own perspective about certain topics but the idea is to line up with God's perspective. Here are some questions to consider to challenge our perspectives. Does masturbating give strength to the spirit or the flesh? Does it keep a person's mind focused on godly thoughts or does it take the mind into a world of fantasy where anything goes? Is there a deeper-rooted issue to resolve like pornography that is driving one to appease him or herself? Have you deceived yourself to believe it's okay to watch other people have sex in porn movies as long as you are not having sex with anyone? Are you a voyeur? Whether you watch it every day, once a week, twice a month or every 3 months it is a serious issue and not God's will. It is unwise to take pornography (lust, voyeurism, orgy concepts, spousal swapping) into God's sacred marital covenant. If you are struggling with this, confess it. Admit to it out loud. Hear yourself confess it. Own it and don't make excuses or justify it. Ask God for forgiveness. Let Him help you to resist and overcome. Let Him cleanse your heart and help you get to the root of your problem as to why you watch it in the first place. He is a faithful healer and will heal you when you admit to it and allow Him to transform your heart and mind. Repentance is intrinsic. Bringing pornography into a marriage will contaminate God's sacred covenant. Talk to God about it (whether you are male or female). He will hear you and deliver you. He's the only one who can.

When one indulges in self-appeasement who is he/she having sex with anyway? At best one is having intimacy with themselves. At worst they are having a moment with an evil lust spirit. On a personal level, have you ever felt a presence in the room or in your bed and there wasn't anyone there but you? Not the presence of God but another presence. A demonic presence. Could it be, masturbation invites an unwanted guest from the dark side of the spirit realm into your room? Is it possible that the only way to get rid of the unwanted guest is to cease from appeasing oneself?

Same-Sex Attractions
Some of you may have been molested as a child and forced to participate in a sexual experience with someone of the same gender against your will. There wasn't anything you could

have done to stop it. It was not your fault. Someone decided to take advantage of your innocence and left you with no other choice but to go along with it and suffer in silence. Since the unpleasant experience you may have been looking to repeat the act because now an attraction for someone of the same gender may be in your system. It's like a drug and you just have a taste for it now. Perhaps your same-sex attraction was the result of a toxic heterosexual relationship that went wrong and was very disappointing. Perhaps it was the result of curiosity or an unexplainable desire.

Regardless of the reason, you can now choose to allow the power of Christ to heal, cleanse, strengthen and restore. Forgiveness is not an easy process but it is possible, doable and healthy for your well-being. You now have the power to choose to allow The Lord to heal you. You now have the power to choose to turn away from the lifestyle. With God all things are possible.

Test Drive the Car?

I understand some people feel the need to test drive the car before buying it. If you know and trust the reputation of the manufacturer, do you really need to test out the vehicle? I know. You just want to make sure the sex is good. Listen, it's possible to have good sex in a bad marriage. It is also possible to have a good marriage with bad sex. Neither one is a healthy outcome. This is why it is important to maintain good communication with the Lord. Could it be that good spiritual intimacy with the Lord is a prerequisite for good physical intimacy with a marriage partner? Is it possible? If this is the case then we wouldn't have to "test" anything out would we? Should we just trust the "goodies" will be good and all will be well in the marital bedroom? Especially since we exercised self- control until the wedding night? Keep in mind that sexual intercourse is God's wedding gift to you. Hmm. Just something to contemplate.

In addition to maintaining good communication with the Lord, It's also important to do and listen to things that give more strength to the spirit than to the flesh. That way you and I will be more alert to make healthier decisions about who we open our hearts up to. We will also be in a better position to overcome feelings of loneliness and lust (which often cause people to "rush" into marriage because the sex is good). Let me also add there is a difference between loneliness and being alone.

Loneliness – To be apart from others or without personal company. A feeling associated with a painful emotional awareness of being alone. To feel an emptiness inside that leads to a need for companionship.

Aloneness – To be apart from others or without personal company. There isn't any painful emotion associated with being alone. The person appreciates companionship but there isn't a need for companionship.

Lust – Perverted desire that seeks to accommodate self and nobody else.

Marriage is not a cure for loneliness or lust. Both of these can open the door to other problems. If we carry these things into a marital covenant they will eventually resurface during the marriage. Why? Because marriage is not a cure for these issues. Loneliness and lust simply open the door to greater problems. These issues can warp our perception of authentic love and can also lead us to get involved in relationships that are merely replicas of what genuine love is.

Nugget of Wisdom

If you trust the name and reputation of the manufacturer, do you really need to test drive the car?

CHAPTER SEVEN
-TRUE LOVE HEALS -

Sexual gratification is a comfort/bondage mentioned in chapter five. Another one mentioned is unhealthy relationships (romantic or platonic). I think it is important to look at different types of relationships that we singles sometimes find ourselves slipping into. You see, we can know who we are in Christ, what we have and what we can do (by His power) and still end up entangled again in a relationship that may not be the best choice for us. In our search for companionship, many times we find ourselves in a disappointing predicament. We love God and yet still have a desire to give love to and receive love from a person. There isn't anything wrong with feeling this way because this is how God designed us. It is only an issue when we place our desire for a human relationship above our relationship with God. A romantic union should always be in addition to our union with God, not in place of.

Before I continue let me just say that relationships are very important to God. We see this truth principle in the Lord's Prayer *(Matthew 6:9)*. Jesus reveals the way to approach God is to address Him as Father. Father denotes relationship (child to a parent). Is Jesus saying in order to approach God we must have a relationship with Him? How can one address God as Father if they do not have a relationship with Him? Could it be that some of our human connections are not successful or healthy because we do not have a successful, healthy connection to God? Is it possible that having a better relationship with a person begins with a better relationship with Him? Hmm. Just something for your spiritual palate to chew on.

Sometimes we have relational problems because many of us don't really know what love is. As mentioned previously, we need a better understanding of what genuine love is and what it isn't. We also need a better understanding of the different types of relationships that can often convey a warped perception of love. We often confuse love with something that may feel like love to us but isn't really love at all. Magazines, romance novels and movies very often portray a superficial, unrealistic, pseudo type of love that can distort our thinking. As I mentioned in chapter six, I was one of those people who thought sex was equivalent to love. When I was intimate with my boyfriend I felt "loved." Growing up I didn't have any genuine examples of love to go by so I couldn't make the distinction. I'm sure I'm not the only one who thought in this manner. I think it is imperative to discuss the difference between a relationship that is founded on love and one that is founded on an imitation or replica of genuine love. As adults, we either search for the love we *did* get growing up or the love we *didn't* get. In fact some of our relationship choices have resulted primarily from an unresolved childhood issue that we were hoping the right relationship would "fix."

In order to continue a celebratory posture in our season of singleness and maintain joy, hope, and freedom it is important to recognize which type of relationship to hope for and which ones are probably best to avoid. There are at least 4 categories of Greek versions of love that may sound familiar to you.

Agape – Supernatural love of God toward mankind developed in us through Christ as we learn how to show toward others.

Storge – Biological love for family especially between parent and child.

Phileos – Platonic love for friends, brothers and sisters in Christ.

Eros – Romantic passionate love for a significant other or spouse.

There are at least six types of relationships that I believe tend to fall under the category of Eros:

Love – a deep, heartfelt emotion that focuses primarily on what can be done to satisfy, please and accommodate the other person and their needs. This genuine love matures into a union that is based on a healthy decision rather than a feeling to continue loving the other person. This authentic love tends to ask this question: How can I be of service to you to amplify your value and accommodate your needs?

Lust – an intense desire that is self-serving and self-focused. It seeks momentary satisfaction driven by unhealthy desire and personal gain that is insensitive to the feelings of the other person; no regard for the other person's needs. Lust adapts the "me, myself and I" syndrome. Although it is very often attributed to things of a sexual nature, it is not only limited to sex. Sexual gratification is the main foundation and cohesive for this type of union. This replica of love tends to ask this question: How can you be of service to me to benefit me and meet my needs?

Infatuation – Usually based on preconceived relationship ideas or a romantic fantasy that is short-lived once reality hits. This is when a person is in love with the "idea" of marriage but not really in love with the other person. They are committed as long as everything is going well. If a relationship hits an inconvenient hiccup (birth of a special needs child, loss of employment, terminal illness, severe accident, change in body weight, etc.) that disrupts their comfort level, the infatuated individual looks for the exit sign. If the physique, beauty, financial status or an image of perfection of the other person is altered the individual leaves the union since there is no other attraction to keep him/her in the relationship. This individual is only willing to stay for the "better" not for the "worse." This replica of love tends to ask this question: How soon can I get out of this relationship because I didn't sign up for this?

Dependency – Based on a constant need for love, affection, attention and affirmation that can at times prove to be emotionally draining or suffocating for the other person. The amount of affection given seems to never be enough. Individual does not feel loved unless they are hearing the other person's voice, seeing their face or experiencing their tangible presence consistently. There is a seemingly unquenchable "emotional thirst." This replica of love tends to ask this question: How can I be happy if the other person doesn't give me more of the love I desperately crave for?

Possessive/Abusive – Founded on a desire to control and dominate the other person who is often seen as property that is owned. Since a person is viewed as an invaluable property he/she is shown very little respect if any at all. Relationships are more of a dictatorship rather than a partnership and many times involve some form of abuse. The extremely insecure abuser (male or female) has problems releasing anger in a healthy manner. Since they lack proper anger management skills, they often resort to verbal or physical violence to express their frustration or dissatisfaction. They often jump to conclusions which only fuels their anger. They gain esteem from bullying others. They maintain superiority by exerting control. The need to feel superior often masks an inferiority complex hidden underneath. Abusers rarely take responsibility for their actions because they don't believe they are at fault for anything. The one being abused is sometimes convinced the abuser really does love them and takes full blame for the irrational behavior. This false concept of love tends to ask this question: How can I convince the other person that if he/she just does whatever I say the relationship will be good?

Obsession – Can be a combination of possessive/abusive and lust but to an extreme that can prove to be dangerous. Individuals are often driven by irrational jealousy, suffocating control and an explosive temper. This imitation of love tends to ask this question: How can I keep the person all for myself, make them love me and promise to always stay and never leave me?

If we do not resolve some of our childhood issues we may

very well find ourselves in one of the latter relationships. Taking these relationship types into consideration, the ideal union would be the one founded on authentic selfless love. As mentioned in chapter one, we have a common pursuit of joy, hope and freedom...even in our relationships. We feel good when we get that uplifting feeling from being around that special someone and hearing their voice. Just thinking about them evokes a tingling, gleeful feeling of excitement. For many of us this is joy. We feel anticipation that the relationship will continue to grow and any issues that arise can be worked out. We look forward to a fulfilling life together. For some of us this is hope. We feel liberated in a union that allows us to be ourselves as the Holy Spirit works on us to produce the fruit of the spirit. We feel free when we can open up about our childhood mistakes and not be judged or condemned by the one who lights up our heart. For some this is freedom.

True joy, hope and freedom is found in our oneness with Christ. It is possible for some of these elements to spill over into our human relationships but it's not going to be easy. All things are possible with God. Not easy. We have to identify those personal issues stemming from our childhood, unmet needs and the issues within our flesh. We should also identify some of those "comforts" we like to turn to that momentarily make us feel better. We are new creations, temples and masterpieces but if we don't deal with our "issues" we will have a hard time being a blessing to a spouse. We will also have a hard time appreciating the spousal blessing who comes into our life. We will find ourselves right back behind bars, stuck in a prison staring at an open prison door. Physically free to go but mentally and emotionally incarcerated.

Marriage comes with its own set of challenges. I believe all humans come with some sought of baggage from the past that has formed us into the adults we are now. I heard a preacher say, "Some of us come with purses. Some with a duffle bag and some with a 5 piece luggage set." We should deal with our own baggage before we take on someone else's. It is hard enough to carry one 30 pound suitcase. Can you imagine dragging two 30 pound suitcases around?

Initially, our joy, hope and freedom should be rooted in our fellowship with Christ. It is intrinsic that we find these wonderful pursuits of life in our relationship with Jesus. Otherwise, we may find ourselves choosing a romantic relationship over our union with the Lord...or getting entangled with one of the imitation relationship types mentioned earlier. If you fit the characteristics of the type of person that would be in one of the "replica" relationships please be honest about any issues you may be struggling with like a quick temper, abandonment, absenteeism, abuse, addictions, neglect, low self-esteem, etc. Primarily, I would suggest seeking the Lord for healing. He is waiting with open arms to embrace you and listen. Secondly, consider reaching out to a licensed counselor who embraces Biblical principles.

Regardless of what type of relationship we find ourselves in we should always be prayerful. Emotion is relevant but we should be led by the Spirit of God, wisdom and discernment when either choosing a mate or agreeing to be someone's mate. This is why the "getting to know you" phase (friendship) is so important. Emotions are necessary but we shouldn't be led by them. Singleness is not about hooking up with someone who fits our "wish" list who we can have a good time with. Marriage is a serious bond and should be seen that way. It's about connecting to someone we have a healthy compatibility with to accomplish the goals God has for our earthly life. God's purposes can be fulfilled through the union. In the interim, we can enjoy each other's company and have a good time! Some people see marriage as a video game or a pair of shoes. A fantasy world of unrealistic expectations or something we can simply exchange or return within 30 days if it doesn't fit. The same way we understand the value and worth of a person we should understand the value and worth of a marital union. If you are presently involved with someone but not quite certain about the relationship I would like to offer a prayer for you.

Lord, may you grant peace to your child and guide him/her in making a correct decision about continuing with this person. Reveal anything that needs to be revealed about the other person. Make it plain so there is no confusion or doubt. Allow your peace to fill his/her heart and saturate their mind. Bring strong confirmation and clarity about what they should do. If he/she needs to let go of the relationship then give him/her the courage to do so. Heal all hurt and disappointment. Rescue him/her from the pain of loneliness. Reassure him/her the best is yet to come. If you give the thumbs up then empower him/her with understanding, wisdom and self-control to continue a successful courtship that will lead to an engagement and marriage. For he/she who has not met that special someone yet continue to embrace them and remind them of your love and that you have not forgotten them. Give them strength to keep holding on to you. Allow them to truly feel your incredible love. Continue to prepare them mentally and emotionally to "become one" with another person in matrimony. Increase hope when they feel weary and ready to give up. Relieve every financial burden and increase wisdom on how to successfully manage funds. Meet every monetary household need according to your abundant, glorious riches. In Jesus' mighty name. Amen.

NUGGET OF WISDOM
**True love heals; a replica of love steals;
character and time reveals as the human heart feels.**

CHAPTER EIGHT
-CAUTION!-

We know who we are, what we have and what we can do. Even with awareness of this truth we are still capable of returning to either a former personal connection or a certain relationship type that does not prove to be very healthy for us. We can also return to an unhealthy habit or pattern of behavior. I have already covered some reasons why we go back to the "prison" (that which is familiar to us or serves as a comfort to us):

- Internal Struggle
- Unresolved Childhood Issues
- Unmet legitimate needs
- Warped concept of what real love is
- Temperament

It is quite a challenge to live for God within a society that does not respect Him. The blatant disrespect for our Creator is shown in some of the laws that have been instituted, some philosophical concepts that are taught in the educational system and some mediums within the entertainment industry. The lack of respect is shown in some of the movies, television shows and videos we watch...and even in some of the music we choose to listen to. Disrespect is also seen in the literature we choose to read which includes social media postings. There are certain "baits" regarding these mediums that can pull us in the direction of temptation which we should be mindful of. Since our adversary is walking around like a roaring lion "seeking whom he can devour" it would be a use of good wisdom to find out what are some of the "baits" that can lead to us being caught up in a trap that can ultimately lead to us being devoured if we don't escape from it.

Here is another reason why we sometimes go back: Door openers.

Door Opener
An audible, visual or tangible apparatus that promotes temptation by triggering the emotions, influencing thoughts, igniting the senses, amplifying insecurities and giving strength to the flesh (appetite for ungodliness).

The short definition for door opener is simply this: a trigger. In chapter two I mentioned we have been given the honor of guarding the entrances to God's temple. Some of these entrances include the eyes and ears. Another word for entrance is gateway. The eyes and ears are gateways to the mind and emotions. Whatever the eyes see or the ears hear will affect our thoughts. Whatever is going on in our thoughts or with our emotions will influence our actions by triggering us to feel a certain way and behave in ways that may not be good.

Let me start off by saying a door opener is not a sin. Some door openers to be discussed are movies, videos, television shows, social media, novels and certain songs. It is not a sin to go to the movies. It is not a sin to listen to non-gospel music. It is not a sin to watch television or partake of social media. What we watch, read or listen to is not a sin issue. It is a flesh issue. These mediums are triggers that give strength to the flesh (the part of us that wants nothing to do with spiritual things or godliness). While these things are *not* sin they can open the door to temptation which can *lead to* sin: Displeasing God.

Growing up my mother was strict but only about certain things. She was strict about taking us to church and giving us a curfew. She was also very strict about not allowing us to entertain company in the house but she wasn't strict about us going to the movies. We were allowed to see "R" rated movies, "PG" rated movies and horror films. We were also allowed to watch television and listen to secular music. I grew up hearing the melodious sounds of Stevie Wonder, The Jackson Five, Michael Jackson, Janet Jackson, Diana Ross, Ohio Players,

Cool and the Gang, K.C. and the Sunshine Band, Taste of Honey, Marvin Gaye, Sugar Hill Gang, Salt-N-Pepa, TLC, Run DMC and the list goes on and on. We could only listen to this music at home though. Not allowed to go to parties. I understand some people didn't have this "leisure" growing up. They were not allowed to go to the movies or watch television. Neither were they allowed to listen to that "devil" music. It was not played in the house. They were raised in a very strict home and attended a very legalistic church that pounded in their heads that these things were sin and they were going to hell if they partook of them.

The adults of former generations were misinformed and didn't have a clear understanding of Bible principles or what it meant to follow Christ. They were good at telling us what not to do but not very good at offering a reasonable explanation of why we shouldn't do it... other than a destination to spend eternity with the devil. This was the only explanation they knew to give. In a naïve, well- meaning effort they were trying to protect their children from the "evils" of society. They just needed a better understanding. That's all.

As I stated earlier the movies we watch and music we listen to are not sin. Nobody is going to hell because they watch an "R" rated DVD or listen to a secular song. Again, it is not a *sin* issue, it is a *flesh* issue. Indulging the flesh opens the door to sin. Romans 13:14 says, "...make no provision for the flesh to fulfill its lusts..." The Amplified Bible says it this way, "put a stop to thinking about the evil cravings of your physical nature to gratify its desires." The New Living Translation words it like this, "Don't let yourself think about ways to indulge your evil desires." Making provision here is synonymous with thinking about something that can lead to an action if we don't put a stop to the thought. Our thoughts can open a door to gratifying the side of us that only wants to bring pleasure to ourselves and not God. This is one reason why we should avoid certain movies, television shows, books, social media postings and songs. They can trigger our thinking (and emotions) and open the door to gratifying sinful desires. How can we put a stop to thinking about the cravings of our flesh if we keep feeding it the things we watch and listen to?

As singles we need to be very mindful of what our eye and ear gates partake of because it will affect how we think and feel. How we think and feel will influence our choices and behavior. Our choices and behavior are a reflection of what we have allowed on the inside through the eye and ear gates. Either we have allowed something in that gives strength to the flesh (appetite for ungodly things). Or we have allowed something in that gives strength to the spirit (appetite for godly things).

*"Walk in the Spirit and you will not fulfill the lust of the flesh.
For the flesh lusts against the Spirit and the Spirit against the
flesh and these are contrary to one another, so that you do not
do the things that you wish."* Galatians 5:16-17

We must be mindful that there is an internal battle happening inside between the appetite for godliness and the appetite for ungodliness. These two forces are constantly fighting against each other. Kind of like the depiction of a little devil sitting on one shoulder and a little angelic angel sitting on the other shoulder, each one trying earnestly to influence our choices. Whichever one we give more strength to will have the upper hand to strongly influence our decisions, conversation and behavior. Whichever one is stronger will determine whether we give in to temptation or are able to resist it. Whatever we open the door to via our eyes and ears will come in. Why is this important? Simply because this can trigger us to slip back into an old habit or relationship that puts us back in a prison. We are responsible for what we allow in.

Watch What You Are Watching
A preacher once said, "Pay attention to what you are paying attention to", "listen to what you are listening to" and "watch what you are watching." I thought this was extremely profound. Whatever we watch or listen to has our attention and

is capable of greatly influencing our choices. Our eyes and ears are entrances or doors to either inspire the Spirit or indulge the flesh. It is important to pay attention to content and lyrics regardless of marital status but especially for those living the single life. The content in R-rated movies (or even some PG-rated films) is not suitable for children but some of it isn't even suitable for adults who have made a decision to live for Christ. Just think about this. If the word of God admonishes us to put off sexual immorality then how are we supposed to do that if we are watching it? God tells us to put off profanity but how can this be done if we are listening to it in a song, comedy show or movie? How can we exercise self-control over our body parts (including the mouth and private parts), anger, jealousy, and gossip if we are entertaining ourselves with secular storylines and lyrics that promote these things? Every movie has a message. Every song has a message. Do the messages contradict the principles in the Bible?

If a single person is challenged with loneliness then it may not be good wisdom to watch romantic love stories. Sometimes these movies can amplify insecurities that you already have about not having a significant other. They can also trigger emotions and thoughts that make you want to be with any-body just to be with somebody. Certain romantic movies can also trigger a desire to watch porn and tempt us to resort to self-appeasement. This is particularly probable if one watches these storylines regularly.

Television used to be wholesome. Nowadays there are things done and said on television that at one time never would have been allowed, especially during primetime. Certain things were censored but now anything goes. There is profanity, partial nudity, explicit bedroom scenes, sexual immorality, raunchy conversations, provocative story lines and rampant disrespect even with some of the cartoon characters. There are some wholesome T.V. shows but not a lot to be entertained by. As an unmarried person it would be wise to be selective about what we watch especially if we are being tempted to get into an emotional or sexual relationship that is not God's best for us.

We should also be mindful of watching movies that are designed to scare us. Scary movies have the propensity to increase fear, anxiety and an inability to sleep well. They can also contribute to disturbing images "stamped" in our minds.

Please stop the music!
Music is an emotional stirrer and evokes a particular feeling. Movies tend to have musical scores to them. If the intent is to make you afraid then the music will be ominous, scary and spooky. If the intent is to make you feel loved then music will

be romantic, heart-stirring and compassionate. If the intent is to produce laughter then music will be giddy, fun and festive. We will feel a certain way. Just like every movie has a message, every song has a message too. What is the message and how does it make you feel when you hear it? What do you find yourself thinking about when you hear a certain song or genre of music? Do you feel like you want to be intimate? Do you feel like you want to give Billy (or Becky) another chance even though you know he/she is not God's best for you? Does the song make you feel more depressed because you are not in a relationship with anyone? Does it make you angry because it reminds you of your ex and now the bitterness is resurfacing every time you listen to the lyrics?

Music also has a strong effect on the spirit realm. What goes on in the spirit realm affects how we feel. We know this truth based on I Samuel 16:14-23. David, anointed by the Spirit of God, was able to drive away a distressing spirit that was tormenting King Saul by playing anointed music on his harp. What do we learn from this? One thing that can be learned is this: anointed music can drive away an evil spirit. So does this mean the opposite is also true? Is it possible that music that is not anointed can attract and invite a distressing spirit to come in? Are some secular songs listened to unintention- ally inviting a distressing spirit of lust, depression, immorality and discouragement into our home, car and lives?

Originally, music was designed to glorify God's character, majesty, power and mighty ability to deliver! Music commemorated His faithfulness and wonderful works of creation! It celebrated His presence and unmatched greatness! His people honored Him with songs of thanksgiving and praise! The angels of Heaven even worshiped Him with awesome wonder and never-ending admiration! Our Creator was worshiped with instruments that constantly resounded in the heavenlies! Before the devil fell from grace, he was involved in the worship whether as a worship leader or angelic participant. He was well aware of the purpose and powerful influence of music. Once relieved of his heavenly duties because of his prideful heart the devil made it his mission to contaminate and pervert everything God created and established which included the music. Instead of honoring what our Father gave us we jiggle what our parents gave us. Instead of drinking in God's presence with His goodness on our mind we are drinking alcoholic beverages with material items on our minds. Wonderful beats to dance to but what is the message? Songs that emphasize body parts, immoral behavior and self-focused activities give strength to the flesh. Indulging the flesh opens the door to sin. Songs that emphasize the body of Christ, godly behavior and the selflessness of the Cross give strength to the Spirit.

Chapter Eight: Caution!

How It All Works

We must know what is happening when we watch a movie, video, play, television show or when we listen to songs. The mind operates like a video recorder or a camera. It records the images on the screen and stores them in the brain (memory). This is why we are able to recall certain scenes from a movie we saw 10 or 20 years ago. The images and scenes are still in our psyche long after the movie is over. We are able to recall and describe parts of the movie because the brain pulls a "snapshot" of the film from the memory bank. The emotions join in with the mind (psyche) and we remember how the movie made us feel (afraid, sad, inspired, angry, happy, lustful, depressed, etc.). Our psyche is connected to the spirit and the spirit to the psyche. The flesh is connected to the psyche and the psyche to the flesh. Many times we are feeling increased depression or loneliness because we are watching and listening to things that give more strength to the flesh (which affects how we think and feel and increases appetite for ungodliness). The next thing you know you may very easily find yourself in an interactive union (relationship) that proves to be very disappointing and emotionally damaging.

You may be thinking to yourself, *"Really? Isn't the only intent of the producers, directors and actors to gross as much money as possible and win an Oscar for best picture? Isn't the only intent of the artist to make people feel good, get a song on the top ten list, have their album go platinum and win a Grammy?"* If you are thinking this you are absolutely correct. I believe in most cases this is the intention...on the surface. But what is going on underneath the surface? Remember, Jesus emphasized there are two existing realms. Earth and spiritual. We do not wrestle against people but against influences of spiritual darkness operating "behind the scenes" and "underneath the surface." The goal of these unwelcome forces is to pull our focus away from Jesus, biblical principles and healthy interactive unions by luring our emotions and thoughts into surrendering to temptation which can cause us to spiral downward to the dungeon of sin and despair.

You and I can watch or listen to whatever we want to but it may not be beneficial to our spiritual growth and emotional healing. *(I Cor.6:12)*. Certain songs and movies are not helpful to our relationship with the Lord. Some are not proper representations of Christ character either. Some songs promote immorality. The lyrics are a direct contradiction to biblical principles and a blatant disrespect to our Creator. There isn't anything wrong with godly entertainment but some forms of entertainment can rob us of true joy, hope, peace and freedom. It would be a good use of good wisdom to be mindful of what our eyes and ears partake of. The Garden of Eden is certain evidence that we can easily be tempted by what we see (fruit) and hear (the influential voice of a serpent). Remember, an influential voice can come through a movie, book, song or conversation with a person. Ephesians 5:18- 19 admonishes us to encourage each other with Psalms, hymns and spiritual songs. This should not only be done during a church service but should be a continuing practice even after the service is over. Why? So our thoughts can stay rooted in Christ. If we want to win the battle over our mind and flesh we will have to adopt the practice of feeding nutritious lyrics to our spirit to help keep it strong.

When the spirit is strong we are better equipped to resist things and people that are not healthy for our well-being. It is beneficial and wise to allow our eyes and ears to partake of songs and movies that:

- Ignite a desire to live for God
- Influence our thoughts with biblical concepts
- Amplify our security in Christ
- Give strength to the spirit

Let's keep inspiring the Spirit and not indulge the flesh! Let's be mindful of mediums that open the door to temptation and pull us out of Christ's character! Let's be diligent gate keepers over our eyes and ears! Let's be mindful that poison into the "gates" can disrupt the soul and disturb the spirit. Let's pay attention to what we are paying attention to, watch what we are watching and listen to what we are listening to!

A Selah moment: Self-reflection thoughts

- Is sexual gratification a "comfort" you struggle with?
- Where in your life is there an open door to be tempted?
- Do the movies you watch and songs you listen to give more strength to the flesh or to the spirit?
- What relationship type do you sometimes find yourself being pulled back into? Why do you suppose?

NUGGET OF WISDOM

**You can't keep the thief out if the
front door is locked but the back door is open.**

Part III

The Prison Door Is Closed:
Living Free and Staying Free

Part III

The Prison Door Swings Open

CHAPTER NINE
-FREE INDEED -

He who the Son sets free is free indeed.
John 8:36

Once the prison door is closed it is imperative that we decide in our heart that we don't want to go back. William McDowell sings a song called, "I won't go back." The lyrics are powerful and should be our anthem. Now this doesn't mean we won't slip up, make mistakes, miss the mark, yield to the flesh and disobey God at times...because we will. A righteous man falls seven times but he will rise again *(Proverbs 24:16)*. We have the propensity to still sin and make bad decisions because the flesh will always contend against us. The spirit is always willing to make right decisions to honor God but the flesh will never yield. The idea is not to live an error free life but to make better choices concerning relationships and all areas of our lives. We want to take necessary measures to maintain joy, hope and freedom during our season of singleness. There are both spiritual and practical measures to take.

This Is How We Live And Stay Free:
Remember who you are
Identify childhood/personal issues
Beware of Door Openers
Set new goals to dissolve old desires
Understand what genuine love is
Recognize relationship types
Share and live the gospel

Remember Who You Are
Constantly remind yourself you are a new creation, a holy temple and a masterpiece! If you have to write it down on index cards and place them around your home so you see it on paper every time you walk in a room then do so. Remembering your identity helps to reaffirm we have the Holy Spirit, the word of God and unlimited access to the throne of God. It is also a reminder we can exercise self –control, live a changed life and turn unhealthy habits into healthy routines. Be honest about the areas where you lack self-control. A lack of control can and will interfere with an ability to live a changed life that is different from the life you used to live before Christ. Make a list of the unhealthy habits you have and how you can turn them into healthy routines. This can pertain to any habit but certainly includes a habit of choosing the

"wrong" person to be in a relationship with. Present your list to the Lord and allow Him to help you make the necessary adjustments.

Perhaps we sometimes attract the wrong person because of how we "advertise" ourselves. When it comes to how we dress in the house of God we want to draw attention to the Lord; not to our wonderfully created body parts. In our everyday attire we want to display self-respect even outside of the house of God. We must be careful how we present ourselves, especially on a date, because we only have one time to make a first impression. If we "advertise the goods" there will definitely be a "buyer" and we may not be able to handle the "price" we have to pay.

Perhaps we sometimes attract the wrong type of person because we are too willing to settle and have not yet embraced our true worth and value. If you really believe you are a masterpiece then do not tolerate anyone treating you like anything less than a masterpiece. You are not a "piece" to be mastered. You are a masterpiece! Remember who you are.

Identify Childhood/Personal Issues

The most challenging thing in life can be identifying our own personal issues. It is so much easier to point out other people's issues. If we are going to live in freedom we must be liberated on the inside. Being locked up in a physical jail is not a good experience but being locked up in an emotional prison is not a pleasant experience either. It is imperative that we identify any of the childhood issues mentioned in chapter five that may still be haunting us as adults. If you need to open up to someone who has a history of being a trustworthy source in your life then do so. You may feel even more comfortable talking to a complete stranger like a licensed Christian counselor. Some of you may only desire to speak to the Lord about those childhood experiences that have contributed to the insecurities we sometimes wrestle with as adults. We can truly be free from the condemnation, inferiority complex, resentment, depression, painful anger, and hard-hearted meanness. These are things that often result from abandonment, abuse, neglect, molestation, being bullied, etc.

If marriage is in your future then now is the time to seek the Lord for healing before entering into a marital covenant. Marriage will not "fix" any of these deep-rooted issues. It will not resolve childhood challenges. In fact, getting married may complicate matters even more and amplify the normal challenges that come with a marriage. Be patient with yourself. Be willing to go through the healing process. Be honest. Identify those personal issues before they identify you.

If you struggle with loneliness or lust, admit it. If you like watching certain movies and TV shows that you know are not appropriate for your eyes to look at then admit it. If the music you like to listen to makes you want to jiggle your stuff more than it makes you want to praise your Father for all He has done for you then admit it. The Spirit of God can help you to be more mindful of the musical selections you are allowing to penetrate your soul and arouse your flesh. Remember, watching movies and listening to songs is not a sin but it can arouse the flesh and once the appetite for ungodly things is aroused it can open the door to sin. Sin is always crouching at the door of the human heart waiting for an opportunity to come in (Genesis 4:7). What is crouching at the door of your heart waiting to gain access?

The first step to freedom is recognizing and admitting that you have an issue or issues. Come out of denial and own it. Turn a mouth of complaint into a mouth of confession. There comes a time in our lives when we have to grow up and stop pointing fingers of blame at everyone else for what went wrong with our lives. Yes it is true that sometimes other people are responsible for some of the childhood issues we have because of the decisions they made that hurt us. Sometimes we are victims of other people's choices and the situation is not our fault. We must learn to forgive and release the anger in a healthy manner so we can be internally free. This can be a progressive process. We must also be willing to move on in our mind and surrender the victim mentality to the Lord so we can joyously celebrate singlehood with a wonderful hope of greater things to come!

Beware of Door Openers

Exhibit wisdom and be mindful about what you allow your eyes and ears to partake of. Bear in mind your spirit, emotions and mental capacity will be affected by it. Don't deceive yourself by thinking you can let just anything into your psyche and not be affected by it. Can a man take hot coals into his hands and not be burned? Whatever we allow can "trigger" our flesh and negatively influence our behavior, actions and choices. We should also be mindful of our alcohol intake. This can also be a trigger. Having a glass of wine is not a sin but we should still use wisdom and exercise self-control. Why? Because liquor has the ability to impair our judgment, influence our behavior and affect our thinking. We should be mindful of drinking wine and strong drink especially if there is a history of alcoholism in our ancestral lineage. We must be wise about what we drink, how much and how often. Perhaps we should not drink at all if the enemy of alcoholism has invaded our family. Even with this in mind, wine should only be consumed in moderation; not to drunkenness. "Do not be drunk with wine but be filled with the Holy Spirit." Ephesians 5:17-18. Our choices should be influenced by the Holy Spirit and not the wine.

We should also be mindful of the reason why we drink alcoholic beverages. Is it a mechanism to help us cope with the challenges of life or unresolved childhood issues? Is it a mask for depression or discouragement? Is your freedom to consume wine causing someone else to stumble? As new creations representing our glorious Savior we can make a choice not to drink alcohol. Let's be an example to others and not a stumbling block. Sparkling cider is a great alternative. These are just some things to consider.

We should also pay attention to the term "wine and spirits." Spirits is just another word for "liquor or strong drink." But consider this. Ever notice how people sometimes act when they get drunk? As if another "spirit" has taken over and is influencing their actions and words. Are we tapping into the demonic spirit realm when we choose to consume strong alcoholic drinks? What are some of the things that trigger an appetite for things that you know you should not partake of? What back door are you leaving open for the enemy to come in and mess you up? Do you want to stay free? Beware of the door openers in your life.

Waiting for a Mate? Set a Goal to Occupy Your Soul!

Setting new goals helps overcome old desires. From a spiritual perspective we need the Holy Spirit, the word of God and self-control to overcome old desires and passions that get us into trouble. Exchange the old unhealthy desire for a new healthy passion. From a practical perspective we need to set some new goals for ourselves. We need something to take our mind off of how long we have been single. I have discovered that when I have a goal to accomplish I don't think about being married or not being married. My mind is not focused on being in a romantic relationship. I pour my mental energy into the goal to be reached (a task God downloaded into me to complete). I wrote down a list of objectives.

For example, writing this book was one of my objectives. The objective became a goal when I attached a date by which to finish it. The book became an accomplishment once it was finished. The second part of the goal was getting it published. Once published this became another accomplishment. Writing down objectives and setting realistic goals feels so good! Turning them into accomplishments feels even better! I would recommend doing the same. Write down your objectives and give yourself realistic dates to finish them by. Whatever steps are needed to take (time set aside, money, people to contact etc.) determine in your heart to be consistent until you do it. Learn to overcome procrastination. In between the goals make sure you have a routine for praying and reading your Word. In the midst of our celebration of singlehood it is imperative that we set new goals to help dissolve old desires.

Understand What Genuine Love Is

Discussions and advice about relationships are very popular these days. It should be because our lives function around our connection to God and to people. The Bible covers relationships from Genesis to Revelation. Interpersonal connections are intrinsic to life. How we relate to God, ourselves and other people is imperative and can often propel or hinder our success. Loving God is our first priority, loving ourselves is our second priority and loving others is our third priority. Jesus said, "Love God with all of your heart, soul, strength and mind. Love your neighbor as you love yourself." How can we love other people if we do not love ourselves first? Very often as singles we are trying to find someone to love us but how can we expect someone else to love us if we don't love us?

Part of maturity is accepting the fact we have issues and we need help to overcome them. I have not experienced the bliss and complexity of marriage yet but this I know. Whatever "love" issues a person has during their season of singleness will come out when they get married. Sometimes we think we can hide things or cover them up but marriage will certainly expose and uncover whatever issue we have. Some issues may not show up while we are dating or engaged (then again sometimes there are red flags that we just simply ignore) but they will definitely show up once we enter into a marital covenant.

That is a guarantee my friend and we will not be able to hide or ignore them anymore.

Before committing to a relationship, make sure you are in love with the person and not merely their gift. I once dated a man who was pursuing me. I was not really attracted to him at all but decided to give him a chance based on a piece of advice received from a friend. He had a powerful prophetic gift that I was drawn to. I was more attracted to his gift than to him. Of course the relationship didn't work because my heart was in the wrong place. There will be a huge problem if you are attracted primarily to anything other than the person's heart and character. You see, when the person's character begins to unravel there will be a serious issue. A person's spiritual gift, money, status, car, well-built body, etc. will not be enough to sustain the relationship. Material things will not be enough to hold a marriage together. What are you attracted to? Be certain the main attraction is the person; not the gift or anything else.

Make sure you love God. Make sure you love yourself BEFORE you vow to love someone else. I'm not talking about a conceited, narcissistic, arrogant self-love. This is not healthy or godly and will only prove to sabotage a marital union. What I am talking about is a healthy esteem, concern, and positive attitude towards oneself that is rooted in Christ. Evaluate where you stand with love. Do you understand what love is? Before you say "I do" ask yourself "Do I?" Do I really love God? Do I show my love for God in how I treat and talk to others? Do I show my love for God in how I live my everyday life? Do I really love myself with a healthy love? Do I really have the desire to love another person the way they need to be loved?

Recognize Relationship Types (see pages 91, 94)

Now, regarding relationship types, it is necessary to identify if you have ever been in any of the unions described in chapter seven. Were you on the receiving end or on the giving end? For example, were you the one being abused or were you the one causing the abuse? Were you the emotionally needy one or was the other person the emotionally needy one? This is not about putting anyone on blast or embarrassing anyone. There is no condemnation to anyone. This is about being honest about where you usually stand in one of these types of unions so you can seek the Lord and get the help you need to truly experience being free, having hope and feeling joy on a regular basis.

A UNION ROOTED IN LUST may consist of a person who is a womanizer, manizer, sex or porno addict who tends to be narcissistic, self-focused, flirtatious with other people and unfaithful. This person doesn't take commitment seriously. They may have a love for money and a lust for material items. This type of person will do anything to get what they want, including compromising morals and the integrity of the relationship.

A UNION ROOTED IN INFATUATION may involve a perfectionist or an individual who has a "white picket fence" mentality. They have preconceived images in their head about how things are supposed to be in a relationship. If there are any deviations from the images in their mind then the personal connection becomes problematic. If the physical appearance, money status, etc. changes then there is no other attraction to their mate. This person may leave abruptly if things are not returned back to the image created in their head.

A UNION ROOTED IN POSSESSION/ABUSE may involve a person who is abusive, controlling, hard to please and narcissistic with anger management issues. Tends to become "god" over the mate.

A UNION ROOTED IN OBSESSION may involve an individual who is jealous, quick-tempered and paranoid with an unreasonable line of thinking. Unwilling to share mates with others like family members and friends.

A UNION ROOTED IN DEPENDENCY may involve a person who is emotionally needy, constantly in need of affirmation, compliments and personal attention. May be fearful of mate leaving and may need three to seven phone calls each day to confirm he/she is loved. Need a huge amount of affection. May not feel loved unless they hear another person's voice, see their face or experience their tangible presence regularly. If they do not feel they are receiving an adequate amount of affection may resort to having an emotional, physical or cyber affair to compensate. Tends to replace God with their mate.

A UNION ROOTED IN GENUINE LOVE involves an individual or two individuals who have made a decision to be committed no matter what comes their way. This person is apologetic and learns to forgive. Also understands that an apology is not always an admission of wrong but at times is a mature and wise means of seeking resolve in the relationship. This person accommodates the other even when the other person does not deserve it or doesn't always return the act of kindness. Affection is selfless, genuine and heart-felt. They agree to disagree amicably and respect each other in public and in private. This person takes responsibility when they say or do something that hurts the other without shifting blame. He/she understands the balance between listening and talking. Constantly answering the question, what can I do for you?

Bear in mind, these descriptions are not limited to the specific types mentioned here but can be interchangeable. For example, the emotionally needy person can have a love for money, the lustful person can be abusive and the infatuated person could be quick tempered.

Sharing And Living The Gospel

Sharing the Gospel with others is a challenge for many. Living it is even more of a challenge. One way to maintain freedom is to focus on sharing the hope of Christ with others. Another way is to allow the Holy Spirit to help us to live the gospel.

Once you get past the fear and nervousness it feels really good to share the hope of Christ with someone who is willing to listen. There were many times I was not sure of what to say but in the moment I opened my mouth to speak the Holy Spirit gave me the words to say. I spoke by His power! Acts 1:8 declares, "But you shall receive power when the Holy Spirit comes upon you and you will be my witnesses, telling people about me everywhere." The unmarried individual should seek to please the Lord *(I Corinthians 7:32 and 34).* Sharing our faith with others definitely pleases the Lord. We can share with others that it is possible to be healed of a broken heart. It is possible to live a refreshing life that puts us at peace with God. People need to know Jesus can free them from habits, addictions, childhood issues and interpersonal connections that prove to be destructive and unhealthy. Instead of using our mouths as weapons of mass destruction we can instead choose to use our mouths as instruments of righteousness! We can share words of hope and love that are rooted in Christ's amazing salvation!

Living the gospel is connected to our behavior. Our behavior is connected to our salvation. Jesus made this truth very clear with certain conversations He had with people *(John 4:13-18, 8:1-11)*. Someone once told me, "people say what they think but they do what they believe." In other words, people say things they do not really believe and their actions show what they really do believe. A nice way of addressing hypocrisy and contradictory behavior. Single community, let us be a people who believe what we say about the gospel and let our behavior show that we believe it!

Putting these things into practice will help us to live and stay free!

NUGGET OF WISDOM
Identify your personal issues before
your personal issues identify you.

CHAPTER TEN
-JOYFUL -

*Joyful is he whose help is the God of Jacob, whose hope
is in the Lord his God, the maker of heaven and earth,
the sea and everything in them; the Lord who remains faithful
forever. He upholds the cause of the oppressed and gives food
to the hungry. The Lord frees the prisoners.*
Psalm 146:5-7

Let's go back to where we started from and tie everything all in. The three main elements focused on are joy, hope and freedom...things I believe we are all in pursuit of. Isn't it wonderful to know our joy and hope is found in the one who frees us?

Joy – Intense, ecstatic pleasure or satisfaction.

Hope – Anticipation and excitement about something good we are expecting to come. A healthy confidence that what we are hoping for will become tangible, visible and experiential to us.

Freedom – To be liberated from an unpleasant situation or released from an oppressive condition

In Chapters 2- 4 we can see the joy released in knowing who we are, what we have and what we can do through our connection to Christ.

In Chapters 5 – 8 certainly there is hope in being able to recognize and identify the factors that many times contribute to a return to the habits and behaviors that are familiar to us and may offer some physical or emotional "comfort." Our hope for change is in the Lord who is our help.

Chapters 9 and 10 truly confirm our reason to celebrate... because we are free! We can see ourselves living a satisfactory, fulfilling life filled with joyfulness, hopefulness and freeness.

We can truly see the freedom in applying biblical principles along with practical principles in order to continuously live and stay free. Living the single life for Christ is a challenge and we need the Lord's help to do it. All things are possible with His power and principles. In our desire to be married let us not forget that marriage is a challenge too. I personally believe marriage should not be a goal but recognized as a gift that should not become a god.

I also believe married life is like climbing a mountain. We need the right equipment. You can't climb a mountain with sandals on. Mountain climbing requires the right equipment, tools and preparatory knowledge. Mountain climbers use special boots, gear and have information about the atmosphere or change in temperature that may occur as they climb higher. Certain information is needed in case possible problems arise like a mountain lion or a bear. The loss of employment, sickness, foreclosure or debt can be some of the "mountain lions" that can arise.

Well the atmosphere of the marriage (time spent together) can change and the temperature (feelings, aspirations) is most certain to change as you "climb higher" in the marriage. A resentful step child, unreasonable ex or difficult in-laws can present some relational challenges that require setting boundaries to promote a successful blended family situation. Having a strong prayer life, biblical principles hidden in your heart and taking pre-marital classes are just some necessary tools that can help. Make sure you have the right equipment before embarking upon the incredible adventure of married life.

Being single is not a curse! It is okay to be single and enjoy it! God does not love us any less. He places the same value on us as He places on all of His children. You have immense value and significant worth. A great masterpiece you are! You are not here just to meander around and take up space. Tap into God's purpose for your magnificent life!

Identify areas where healing and transformation is needed. Allow the Lord to be the salve for your delicate heart and the balm for your emotional scars. Set some realistic goals with some realistic deadlines! Be mindful to feed your spirit more than the flesh. Watch out for door openers! You are not crazy. You are not weird. You are in a battle between flesh and spirit. Use the essentials God has given you (Holy Spirit, Word and unlimited access) to overcome the challenges you face.

Bond with another single friend who is on the same spiritual page you are on. This is important: you should be mindful of the company you keep because bad company corrupts good morals. People who do not have the same spiritual focus can be more of a hindrance than a help. Connect yourself to people who have a healthy desire to grow, a mature heart to change, and are going in the same direction you are. Pray for each other. Pray with each other. Encourage one another. Support each other's goals, gifts, ideas, aspirations and divine purpose! Let us unite single people! We are a community! We are family! We are in this thing together!

Stop mourning being single and rejoice in your single status! Take off the grave clothes of gloom and discouragement. Put on the garments of praise and celebration! The joy of the Lord is our strength! In His presence is full complete joy! Let your heart be glad! Let your mouth rejoice and your body will live in hope! The Lord has freed us! Celebrate your freedom!

We always celebrate marriage. Let's celebrate singleness too! We may not be engaged yet but we can celebrate our engagement with the Lord and His promise to take care of us! We may not be able to celebrate a wedding day yet but we can celebrate the day we were joined to the Lord in a wholesome spiritual relationship at the spiritual altar! We may not be celebrating the honeymoon yet but we can celebrate every "honeymoon experience" we have had with the Lord in our intimate time of devotion to Him! We can celebrate every time He came through for us when we needed His help, guidance AND PROVISION! Shout Hallelujah for His never-ending love!

Let's stay focused on Jesus so we don't end up in a wrong relationship, marrying the wrong person for the wrong reasons with a wrong concept of what love is. Embrace the wonderful single life of sharing your heart with Jesus who remains faithful forever! He is our hope to lift up the oppressed, give spiritual food to the hungry and free those in an emotional prison. He is our Shepherd taking good care of us and shall continue to do so! The neighborhood of singlehood is really good!

When you and I have a different perspective we can sincerely see a reason to celebrate our spectacular purpose-filled lives! Rejoice in the fact you have the Lord to help you overcome personal issues! Rejoice in the fact you have an amazing Lord with amazing love for you! Who is the one who forgives us every time we make a mistake or step out of Christ's character? The Lord. Celebrate Him!

Celebrate being a magnificent masterpiece, a terrific temple and an awesome new creation! Celebrate that you have God's spirit, His word and unlimited access to His impeccable throne!

Celebrate that no matter how much we have messed up in the past or the present we can still live a changed life with self-control!

Dance unto the Lord because He has great things in store

for your life! Shout unto the Lord because there is immeasurable hope for all of us! Sing because the Lord is your help! Celebrate singleness!

Freedom + Hope = Joy!

Joyful is the one who is filled with hope because the Lord has freed the prisoners!

NUGGET OF WISDOM

You can't sell the house if the exterior looks great but the interior needs to be renovated.

EPILOGUE

Here is a list of inspiring, encouraging and empowering music that helps me get through some challenging moments on this amazing single journey. I hope these songs can be as beneficial to you as they are to me.

ARTIST	SONG
Anointed	*Anything Is Possible*
BeBe & CeCe Winans	*Can't Take This Away*
	The Blood (ft. MC Hammer)
Tasha Cobbs	*Break Every Chain*
Mary Mary	*Can't Give Up Now*
Fred Hammond & RFC	*I Press*
Kenoly Brothers	*Why I Love You (You Are My Joy)*
Jonathan McReynolds	*Make Room*
	Great Is The Lord
	Not Lucky, I'm Loved [live video]
Todd Dulaney	*Victory Belongs to Jesus*
	Psalm 18
Travis Greene	*Made A Way*
J.J. Hairston	*Lord You're Mighty*
VaShawn Mitchell	*Nobody Greater*
Vickie Winans	*Shake Yourself Loose*
Tamela Mann	*Take Me To The King*

Celebrate Freedom

Artist	Song
Sinach	*Way Maker*
	I Know Who I Am
Vicki Yohe	*Because of Who You Are*
Yolanda Adams	*The Battle is the Lord's*
Richard Smallwood & Vision	*Anthem of Praise*
Israel & New Breed	*You Are Good*
	Again I Say Rejoice
Israel Houghton	*Saved By Grace*
	I Receive
	Moving Forward

Artist	Album
CeCe Winans	*Greatest Hits*
Shekinah Glory Ministry	*Praise is What I Do*
New Life Community Choir ft. John P. Kee	*Show Up!*
Richard Smallwood	*Adoration*
Kari Jobe	*Kari Jobe*
Brooklyn Tabernacle Choir	*I'll Say Yes*
Donnie McClurkin	*Live in London And More*

Hymns: *Pass Me Not, Oh Happy Day*

CALL TO SALVATION

If you confess with your mouth that Jesus is Lord and believe in your heart that God raised Him from the dead you will be saved.

It is with your heart you believe and with your mouth you confess and are saved.

Repent and be baptized in the name of God the Father, Jesus Christ His Son, and the Holy Spirit.